PLAIN TALK
ABOUT
THE HOLY SPIRIT

PLAIN TALK
ABOUT
THE HOLY SPIRIT

Manford G. Gutzke

BAKER BOOK HOUSE
GRAND RAPIDS, MICHIGAN

Contents

1

Paul's Benediction

II Corinthians 13:14

Have you ever wondered whether the Bible speaks of the Holy Spirit as a person in Himself?

> The grace of the Lord Jesus Christ, and the love of God, and the communion of the Holy Ghost, be with you all. Amen (II Cor. 13:14).

These words are commonly called the Apostolic Benediction. In the practice of the church, this is often considered a very special benediction and in some denominations only an ordained minister will use it. These words are very important because they convey so much. If you will remember these words just as I have quoted them, you will notice that there were three principal words: *grace, love, communion*. They are often loosely interchanged, yet they are very different in their ideas.

> For ye know the grace of our Lord Jesus Christ, that, though he was rich, yet for your sakes he became poor, that ye through his poverty might be rich (II Cor. 8:9).

This is what is meant by the grace of our Lord Jesus Christ. It is a matter of His taking what He has and giving it for those that He had in mind. The expression "the grace of our Lord Jesus Christ" refers to something which He gave to His followers, to His believers. As a matter of fact, the New Testament makes it very clear that Jesus of

7

Nazareth gave His earthly body. When you speak of "the grace of our Lord Jesus Christ," you are referring to receiving something from Christ that you need but could never earn.

> For God so loved the world, that he gave his only begotten Son, that whosoever believeth in him should not perish, but have everlasting life (John 3:16).

The word "love" as used in the New Testament, especially when referring to the love of God, has very little to do with sentiment. This phrase does not say how God felt, it says how God *is*. Love in the New Testament is an action verb. It does not refer to feelings. There are words like "compassion" and "pity" that refer to feelings. But when the word "love" is used in saying "God so loved the world," that does not mean that He was all inwardly aglow when He looked at the world. Actually the word "love" points to the direction of the action. "God so loved the world" means He had such an attitude toward the world that He gave His only begotten Son. Not that He was delighted or that He was pleased or that He was inwardly elated; nothing like that. He "gave his only begotten Son," in order that "whosoever believeth in him should not perish but have everlasting life." The expression "the love of God" does not mean His kindly feeling. It does not mean His affectionate regard. It does mean what He will do for you in Christ Jesus, viz., that He would give His Son to die for you. John, in his first epistle, says, "Herein is love, not that we loved God, but that he loved us, and sent his Son to be the propitiation for our sins."

"And the communion of the Holy Ghost be with you all." The word "communion" draws attention to a very close personal fellowship. Jesus of Nazareth promised: "For if I go not away, the Comforter will not come unto you; but if I depart, I will send him unto you" (John 16:7). All through that portion of the Gospel of John it was clearly pointed out that when Jesus of Nazareth had been glorified, when He had been taken up into the presence of God as the Son of God, He would send the Holy Spirit as the Comforter. The Holy Spirit, coming into the hearts of believers, would activate in them a communion with God.

These three words, *grace, love,* and *communion,* are contained in this Apostolic Benediction and reveal something of the significance of the Holy Spirit. Paul wants believers to share in the threefold blessing from the Triune God. "The grace of the Lord Jesus Christ, the love of God, and the communion of the Holy Spirit." The Bible sees all three aspects of the blessing of God in one perspective. This is one of the places in the Bible where it is to be seen that the Father, the Son, and the Holy Spirit are spoken of as three different persons. Another such passage is:

> . . . and, lo, the heavens were opened unto him, and he saw the Spirit of God descending like a dove, and lighting upon him: And lo a voice from heaven, saying, This is my beloved Son, in whom I am well pleased (Matt. 3:16-17).

This clearly reveals the truth that the Holy Spirit of God is a person, just as God the Father is a person, and God the Son is a person. The Holy Spirit is one of three persons. Some would say that the phrase "Father, Son and Holy Spirit" refers to three different aspects of one person. But close attention to this passage refutes such interpretation. "The heavens were opened unto him"—that would be unto John the Baptist—"and he saw"—John saw—"the Spirit of God descending like a dove and lighting upon him"—on Jesus of Nazareth. This is the record that the Spirit of God was coming down and lighting upon Jesus of Nazareth. "And lo a voice from heaven, saying, This is my beloved Son, in whom I am well pleased." It is plainly obvious this account reveals three persons involved. Jesus of Nazareth is there in the body, and being baptized by John the Baptist. A voice from heaven is saying, "This is my beloved Son." This is the way the Bible puts it, and while men have tried to explain the Trinity over and over in various ways, the record is clear that these three persons exist at the same time and are different from each other. A simple statement like this leaves no room for question or doubt about the teaching of Scripture.

The Holy Spirit is a person. He does not have a body as we do, that is true! He is a Spirit. And in this He is like God the Father or like angels: He is a person. He has the capacities of thought and feeling and will. The Spirit can be grieved like a person can be grieved; and the Spirit divides the various gifts severally as He will. This is action as on the part of a person. He is one of the three persons of the Godhead, and as such He is equal in power and in might and in glory with the other two. He is referred to in the Bible as God, as one of the three persons of the Godhead. When we speak about the Holy Spirit being in a person, we mean that this is God in that person. When we speak about receiving the Holy Spirit of God, we mean we are receiving the presence of God. The truth is that God the Father is in heaven, and God the Son is at the right hand of God the Father; but the Holy Spirit is now in the world with the believer.

In the Apostolic Benediction "The grace of the Lord Jesus Christ, and the love of God, and the communion of the Holy Ghost be with you all," the word "Ghost" is used in referring to the Spirit. In the original language there was no difference between the two. The word "ghost" and the word "spirit" meant the same thing, an entity that does not have a material body. We should remember that the Holy Spirit is God: one of the three persons of the Godhead. To speak about receiving the Holy Spirit is to speak about receiving the very presence of God.

2

The Believer's Need for the Holy Spirit

Romans 7:14-25

Would you understand why the Holy Spirit is necessary in the life of a believer? If anyone were to ask, Why was it necessary for Christ

Jesus to come and to die, could you answer? A believer would say, "I was lost. I was dead in trespasses and sin," and he would quote Scripture to say "The Son of man is come to seek and to save that which was lost." Why is it necessary that the Holy Spirit should be working in a person? Why is it absolutely necessary that the believer have the Holy Spirit? Because man needs help to do the will of God.

That men are not doing the will of God is easy to recognize but it is oftentimes not understood just why this is so. Why do people not obey God? Some probably think that the reason people do not obey God is because they are ignorant, and persons who believe this will try to learn for themselves and educate others, the result being that much activity carried on in the name of the gospel and in the name of the Lord Jesus Christ is in the nature of an information bureau. The aim seems to be to tell people things which it is assumed would enable them to change their ways.

Others seem to think that the reason men do not do the will of God is lack of motive, that they just do not want to. So these people seek to inspire men in various ways. There are generally two ways to inspire a person to act. One aims to instill fear by telling people the hard things that will happen to them if they fail to act, emphasizing that they would be in real danger of suffering calamity if they did not do something. This is one way. Another way to inspire motive would be to give promises of benefits to be received. If such and such a thing is done, certain good things will follow.

Some seem to feel that the reason men do not do the will of God is lack of opportunity, and so they try to provide such opportunity. The idea that if people were living under fortunate circumstances they would do the right thing is to assume that human beings want to do the right thing, but are hindered because circumstances are against them. But that is really a false assumption.

Each one of these ideas points in a direction that is sound enough so far as it goes, and may have enough validity so that it is true to a certain extent. Perhaps ignorance does make a difference, and no doubt lack of motive makes a difference, just as lack of opportunity would make a difference, yet none of these recognize the heart of the matter. The truth of the matter is "there is none good, no, not

11

one." The real truth of the matter is that man, as a human being, as a natural person, as a child of Adam, cannot do the will of God and does not want to do the will of God. Even if a man knew what to do, naturally he would not want to do it. Even if he had opportunity to do it, he would not want to do it. It is easy for a believer to be mistaken at this point. By the grace of God, the believer is converted to a new frame of mind, and because he has a new frame of mind and has new ideas, he cherishes new hopes and new aims. The believer can be tempted to think that now that he will want to go in the right direction, and that he can do it. This is not true. The sad truth is that even if he wants to, he cannot.

Paul describes the situation clearly:

For we know that the law is spiritual: but I am carnal, sold under sin. For that which I do I allow not: for what I would, that do I not; but what I hate, that do I" (Rom. 7:14-15).

In the phrase "that which I do," the Greek word brings out the idea of "practice." Paul is saying, "What I customarily practice, 'I allow not.' I do not approve it myself. I am not in favor of acting like I act. But 'what I would,' what I really want to do, 'that do I not.' I just do not practice the very thing I really want to do. 'But what I hate,' the very kind of thing I am against, 'that do I.' " How many times a person will think to himself when the day is over: "Why did I spend that money over there? I do not really want to spend my money that way, but I did. Why do I waste so much time as I do? I do not want to waste my time. But I do!" This situation is often seen in college and university. Students pay room, board, buy books, and then will not study. They want to study, they mean to study, but they do not do it. Paul reveals the reason. " 'If then I do,' if I practice, 'that which I would not,' that is, what I do not want to, 'I consent unto the law that it is good.' " This is a way of saying, "I am in favor of what is right and I know what is wrong." "Now then it is no more I that do it but sin that dwelleth in me. For I know that in me, that is in my flesh (in my human nature) dwelleth no good thing." That is the way Paul put it. "For to will is present with me; but how to perform that which is good I find not." He could make up his mind to do right and then turn right around and do the opposite. " 'For the good that I would,' what I really want to do, 'I do not,' I do not practice it. 'But the evil which I would not, that I do.' " Paul concludes by exclaiming "O wretched man that I am! who shall deliver me from the body of this death?"

It would help to circle the word "I" everywhere it occurs in Romans 7, verse 14 to 25. These little circles will appear all through the passage. Then go on in chapter 8, and as you read through that, underscore or circle the word "Spirit." The result will be amazing and revealing. In chapter 7 you will find "I," "I," "I" and the word "Spirit" is not mentioned; but in chapter 8, there is no "I" at all, but "Spirit," "Spirit," "Spirit." This is very significant. Paul points plainly to the truth of the operation of the Holy Spirit.

> But if the Spirit of him that raised up Jesus from the dead dwell in you, he that raised up Christ from the dead shall also quicken your mortal bodies by his Spirit that dwelleth in you (Rom. 8:11).

Any man in himself, even a good man, is not good enough and he is not strong enough. He is not even willing enough to do the will of God. And if anyone, despite his best intentions, has found that his own heart does not obey him, and does not find himself turning to God, he can see that he needs help. And this is why the Holy Spirit is given. "Likewise the Spirit also helpeth our infirmities" (Rom. 8:26).

3

Christic Jesus Sends the Spirit

John 14:15-16

Do you realize that the Holy Spirit is available only for believers? No matter how often it is stressed in our Bible reading and in Bible teaching that *it is "Christ in you" that is the hope of glory,* it is so natural for the believer to give himself credit for his conduct and take glory to himself. This is unfortunate. Because when he thinks this way, the believer assumes a load which he cannot carry, and a task that he cannot perform.

If I were a believer, and yesterday my neighbor acted in a way that would ordinarily have provoked me, and instead of my trying to get even with him, I found it in my heart to forgive him, to be meek about it and not to retaliate, as a believer I would realize this was the result of the Holy Spirit activating in my heart the mind and the will of Jesus Christ. But if I were not careful, I could think I did it and so feel that I am that good. Then I would find myself not trusting in the Lord but trusting in myself. Any time a believer acts that way he can expect real trouble in days to come, for he will neglect to seek the help of the Lord as he lives. It is a common error to assume that the believer has done what he has done in his own strength, and because he has, he can now be an example that others can follow.

Often in Sunday school and church young people are taught over and over again they ought to be good, kind, and loving. All the different virtues of the believer are held out before them and then each believer is told that this is what he ought to do. All of this advice is based on the assumption that he could if he wanted to. But he cannot.

The Lord Jesus plainly taught His disciples in John 14, 15, and 16 the truth of what He was going to arrange. In this extended passage is the promise about the Comforter, the Holy Spirit, whom the Lord Jesus Christ will send. Sometimes it is written:

> And because ye are sons, God hath sent forth the Spirit of his Son into your hearts, crying, Abba, Father (Gal. 4:6).

The Holy Spirit has been sent into the heart of the believing person that He might activate in that person the will of the Lord Jesus Christ.

This is a truth we cannot expect the world to accept or to believe. Let us consider what happens with electric extension cords. We plug one end into the wall socket, the other into the cord of an appliance, flip a switch, and operate the appliance. Someone might ask, "How?" We understand there will be power going through the cord. Now look at the cord. Do you ever see anything passing through there? Do you see any bulge going along that cord? Is there any visible evidence? Is the cord changed? If you were to open up the cord, is the copper in there any different than it was before?

When the cord is not plugged into the socket, it is just a cord. All you could do with that cord would be to tie up a package. Yet the cord is of such a nature that if you put one end of it into the socket that attaches it to the dynamo, and the other end of it into the appliance, power will make that machine run.

This is exactly how the unbelieving world might look at the Bible. To many people, the Bible is just a book. Often when I have seen people carrying a Bible, I think to myself, someone is carrying around an armful of electric cords which need only to be plugged in to be powerful. And this is far too often the truth about the lives of believers. Nothing happens that would show the power of God. There are no results in the life. The Holy Spirit is not operative. If the believer were by faith hooked up to the promises of God, to God Himself, and if he were committed to obey in his heart, so that the promises of God would affect his heart, something would surely happen! The Lord Jesus said, "Abide in me and I in you." If any man will abide in Him, so that the Lord abides in that man, the same will bring forth much fruit. The presence of Christ dwelling in the

15

heart by faith is possible only by the Holy Spirit of God. Christ sends the Holy Spirit into the heart to accomplish things in the believer just like electricity going through the extension cord will make an appliance work.

Christ Jesus sends the Holy Spirit to be an ever-present Companion and Comforter to the believer (John 14:16-18).

> . . . he shall teach you all things, and bring all things to your remembrance, whatsoever I have said unto you (John 14:26).

When the believer is right with God and lets God work in him, this is what is going to happen. The Holy Spirit will work in him and cause him to bring "forth much fruit." Christ Jesus sends the Holy Spirit into the heart of His people to accomplish things.

The Holy Spirit has a broad function to perform.

> And when he is come, he will reprove the world of sin, and of righteousness, and of judgment (John 16:8).

John goes on to say: "He will guide you into all truth . . . He will shew you things to come. He shall glorify me: for he shall receive of mine, and shall shew it unto you." In fact John 14, 15, and 16 reveal much about the work of the Holy Spirit. This portion of Scripture gives a clear revelation that Christ Jesus sends the Holy Spirit into the heart of His believing people that He might work in them to will and to do the good pleasure of God.

4

The Spirit Sets the Believer Free from the Flesh

Romans 8:1-4

Did you know that the great blessing of a Christian is to be set free from the longings, desires, and appetites of human nature? A Christian has in him actually two power systems. As a child of his parents he is human, a natural being. As a believer, he is born again as a child of God and thus has a spiritual nature in him. The Bible reveals the difference between being a child of Adam and being a child of God. Some people in their kind eagerness would like to say that everyone created by God is a child of God. The Bible does not say that. A creature of God, yes, but not a child. What the Bible does say is:

> He came unto his own, and his own received him not. But as many as received him, to them gave he power to become the sons of God, even to them that believe on his name (John 1:11-12).

The Bible shows there is in man two different natures. The "natural" he received when he was born of his earthly parents, and the "spiritual" when he was regenerated, born a child of God. Paul calls the first "flesh," the second "spirit." It is common thought that the flesh is all bad, but as far as the flesh is concerned, one can say there is both good flesh and bad flesh. All civilization is a refinement of the flesh. There is culture and refinement and vulgarity; decency and crudeness. Paul would call anything physical, mental, or in any way involved in human beings "the flesh," the natural. In contrast is the spiritual, when one is a child of God by being regenerated, born again; when one is brought alive by the life of God within him, which is eternal life.

All of this is implied in Romans 8:1-4:

> There is therefore now no condemnation to them which are in Christ Jesus, who walk not after the flesh, but after the Spirit. For the law of the Spirit of life in Christ Jesus hath made me free from the law of sin and death. For what the law could not do, in that it was weak through the flesh, God sending his own Son in the likeness of sinful flesh, and for sin, condemned sin in the flesh: That the righteousness of the law might be fulfilled in us, who walk not after the flesh, but after the Spirit (Rom. 8:1-4).

Paul is making a distinction between those who walk after the flesh and those who walk after the Spirit. Following "the law of the Spirit of life in Christ Jesus" means a characteristic way of being and doing in which the Spirit of life in Christ Jesus operates in the believer, making the believer free from the characteristic way in which sin and death operate. The flesh and the Spirit are opposites, just as water and fire are opposites. Water, for example, runs down; fire goes up. Water tends to be cool; fire is hot. They cannot both be in the same place. However, put water in a kettle and set it over a fire and the water in the kettle becomes steam and it becomes vapor. And how does it act? It acts just like fire. It does not go down like water; it goes up like fire. The water is not really changed. If it should get away from the heat and cool off, if would become mist and fall right back to the ground. Then it would act just as it did before.

So it is with faith. A person may be profoundly affected spiritually, so that he actually turns to God. His life may be outwardly changed. After a period of time that person may do again the things he used to do. He falls right back to where he was before. Someone may say, "It just did not do him any good," but becoming a believer does not make an angel out of the believer. No. His experience is like that of water. While the water had the power of the fire in it, the heat in it, it went up and acted like fire. But it was not fire. It was water all the time, even though it acted like fire. This is the way it can be with a professed believer. He is still human, even though the power of the Holy Spirit may be operative in him. He can be lifted up so that he lives and walks and acts as if he were actually a son of God. This is what he now is, and this is how he will be made to act.

Another example will help. If I pick up a pencil and then release the pencil, it will fall. If I hold the pencil, and move it, it will move because of me. That is the way it is with a believer. Christ Jesus takes hold of him, lifts him, and moves him. The pencil does not have in it the power to be lifted or to move and to draw and to write. It is the hand that does the work. That is the way it can be with the believer. He can be lifted, freed from earthly things by God's hand.

The Spirit of Christ, the Spirit of life in Christ Jesus "hath made me free from the law of sin and death." The Holy Spirit of God can move me today in my home, in my office, in my school. He can move me into the will of God, move me to do the will of God, setting me free from natural desires and natural inclinations. I do not have to be myself: I can be in Christ Jesus; and I can have Christ Jesus in me. That is "the hope of glory."

5

The Carnal Mind Is Enmity Against God

Romans 8:5-8

Have you ever realized that any human being as such is just naturally opposed to the ways of God? A person can know the wonderful privilege of being a Christian. A person can have the power of God in his life. Paul in analyzing the experience and conduct of any believer named two elements, flesh and spirit. Paul meant by the flesh everything that is natural, and by the spirit all that is spiritual. In the one the person is a child of Adam, in the other he is a child of God; the one is human, the other is spiritual. Paul had this in mind when he wrote:

> For they that are after the flesh do mind the things of the flesh; but they that are after the Spirit the things of the Spirit. For to be carnally minded is death; but to be spiritually minded is life and peace. Because the carnal mind is enmity against God: for it is not subject to the law of God, neither indeed can be. So then they that are in the flesh cannot please God (Rom. 8:5-8).

Paul recognized that there are two ways of living, just as there are two ways of moving a boat across the lake. One can row across with oars or one can attach a motor and go across effortlessly. There are also two ways to get to the top of a building. One can climb the stairs or one can ride the elevator. Paul examined these two ways of living, flesh and spirit, and noted the difference. When he said "they that are after the flesh," he meant to say their thinking is according to their own ego, personal feelings, and desires. This is natural man. "And they that are after the Spirit." These words refer to the born-again ones, those who now belong to Christ Jesus, whose consciousness is controlled by the will of Christ. It was in this context that he wrote that the "carnal mind is enmity against God."

The carnal man, the natural man, the big "I," is opposed to the spiritual. As self-preservation is the first law of nature, self-denial is the first principle of the Spirit. These are opposite. The natural way to preserve self is enmity against God: it is opposed to, contrary to, against, just the opposite of the ways of God. This point can perhaps most readily be recognized when one looks at the life of Jesus of Nazareth. Jesus of Nazareth most likely never developed a personal ego. In the Gospels, Matthew, Mark, Luke, and John, are the things reported about Jesus of Nazareth. There is no record of Him talking about Himself, about anything He wanted to do. He said, "I do always the things that please my Father." The contrast between the carnal and the spiritual is doing what I want to do or doing what God wants me to do.

Generally speaking, when people use the word *carnal*, they mean something ugly and dirty. Paul did not mean it that way; he used the word carnal as meaning *of the flesh*. He could have used the word *human*. One effect of the Holy Spirit would be to reverence God, and this would mean that a spiritual person would read his Bible and pray. The carnal mind would be against that. The natural man, the ego, the self has no time to read the Bible or to pray. Another thing the Spirit would prompt the believer to do would be to respect those in authority. Such a person would obey the traffic rules. He would not need to have a policeman watching him all the time. The spiritual man would remember those things, and when he parks, or drives, he would go according to regulations. Now what would the natural man, the carnal man, the ego-involved person be inclined to do? In traffic he would want to take every advantage; he would want to get there first. This is the natural, the carnal, and it is definitely different.

God wants a person to be considerate of other people. Paul writes to the Philippians, "Look not every man on his own things, but also on the things of others." When a believing person starts out the day, he will be thinking in terms of the comfort of other people. If a person comes into an office and finds the air stuffy, what will he want to do? If he were thinking in the way in which the Lord would have him think, he would be asking himself, How do the folks here feel? Is this comfortable for other people? If he were a natural, carnal person how would he feel? "I feel hot." Then without thinking of others, he would go and swing open the door, or raise the window.

This can also be seen in the matter of sharing, of giving to the poor. The Lord would have a person give to the poor: "Whoso asketh of thee, turn him not away." What would the carnal man think? "I have nothing to give, for I need it all myself. I need everything I have. I need all I can get." The natural heart is enmity against the things of God.

6

The Essential Role of the Spirit

Romans 8:9

Do you understand that living as a Christian is impossible apart from the actual operation of the Holy Spirit from within? Perhaps you have not yet begun living the life of faith, and perhaps so far as you are concerned you do not even understand all that is involved. I hope that you will read prayerfully what I have to say to Christian people about the provision that is made for them in the Holy Spirit. Paul wrote very plainly to his people when he said:

> But ye are not in the flesh, but in the Spirit, if so be that the Spirit of God dwell in you. Now if any man have not the Spirit of Christ, he is none of his (Rom. 8:9).

These studies focus attention upon the truth of the Holy Spirit as it is revealed in the Bible. Many teachers have talked about the Holy Spirit, setting forth their ideas. What is most important, however, is what the Bible teaches about the Holy Spirit, the third person of the Godhead, a person who is alive and, since Pentecost, is in the believer.

The plan of God is that whosoever will believe in the Lord Jesus Christ will be saved by the power of God. If anyone were to ask, "How do Christians say they are saved?" the answer would be, "Through Jesus Christ." Then if someone were to ask, "If a soul wanted to be saved according to the Christian gospel, what would he do?" the answer would be, "Believe in the Lord Jesus Christ." That understanding is very important, and basic to the Christian witness. The simple truth is that whosoever believes in the Lord Jesus Christ shall be saved. The sinner must believe in the Lord in order to receive the Holy Spirit. Something must start happening in him and in accordance with what he believes.

In the prophecy of Ezekiel is described the vision Ezekiel had when he was shown a valley of dry bones. He saw himself called upon to preach to those dry bones. When he preached to them there was a great noise and a great fluttering; and those bones came together and formed the structure of a person. Then they were covered with sinews and with flesh until the body of a person developed. But in his vision, in his dream, this body was not alive. He had done the preaching and as a result this body appeared, all built together with bones and muscles, but it was not alive. Then he was told to prophesy to the wind. This seems to mean that he was to pray for the Holy Spirit, and then, lo and behold, in his vision, this person became alive.

There is much implied in this vision that fits the gospel. Knowing the gospel, knowing the form of it, as important as that is, is not enough. The hearer must yield to the guidance of God. The Holy Spirit must come into the heart and begin to operate there. He must make the will of God known and felt from within. "Ye are not in the flesh, but in the Spirit, if so be that the Spirit of God dwell in you." This passage reveals that when the Spirit of God dwells within the heart, He will overcome the flesh. So it follows that when the Spirit of Christ dwells within a person, that person is no longer in the flesh, is no longer motivated by human considerations but by the spiritual considerations of the presence of God. When the Spirit of Christ dwells in the heart, the things of the flesh are no longer operative because the Spirit controls. This can be more clearly understood when it is noted what the Spirit does.

One does not smell the Spirit like a perfume, nor feel the Spirit like a wind. The Holy Spirit brings to the consciousness the truth of the Lord Jesus Christ: that He died for sins, was buried, arose, and is alive now! The Spirit will not be given to any person unless he believes these facts. If one does not believe that Christ Jesus died for him, and has called him to trust in God, to receive the Holy Spirit, he would never have the Holy Spirit. God gives the Holy Spirit to whosoever believes in the Lord Jesus Christ. The Spirit will remind the soul of the crucifixion and resurrection of Christ. Just as surely as the believer accepts and receives Jesus Christ as presented in the gospel, the Spirit is given. The wonderful truth is that anyone can come, and whosoever will come, God will in no wise cast out; and "whosoever believeth in Him shall not perish but have everlasting life." All of this is most important and reveals plainly that no human being can in himself live as a believer. It is a pathetic sight to see someone in all the goodness of his heart trying to live like a Christian. Brother, it cannot be done, not in your own strength. Sister, you will just wear out. Yield; let Christ live in you. He can do it in you and for you. People are born as human beings. They live in the flesh naturally. Living in the flesh, they can be civilized: they can be refined, they can be disciplined, they can be educated, but they will always be sinful. They will always be ego-centered and they will always be unacceptable to God. But souls who receive Christ Jesus by denying self, by being regenerated by the power of God and receiving the Holy Spirit are lifted to a higher plane. That is why Paul says, "Ye are not in the flesh, but in the Spirit, if so be that the Spirit of God dwell in you." That will surely happen if you are a believer. "If any man have not the Spirit of Christ, he is none of his."

7

The Power of the Holy Spirit

Romans 8:10-11

Have you ever realized that the power at work in the life of a Christian is the same power that raised Jesus from the dead?

And if Christ be in you, the body is dead because of sin; but the Spirit is life because of righteousness. But if the Spirit of him that raised up Jesus from the dead dwell in you, he that raised up Christ from the dead shall also quicken your mortal bodies by his Spirit that dwelleth in you (Rom. 8:10-11).

Being a Christian is not a matter primarily of being a good person, but being a person in whom God is operating to bring His will to pass through Christ Jesus. Human beings differ—some are good, some bad, some good for nothing. There is not a single human being able to do God's will in himself. The Christian is a human being who has surrendered himself to God through Christ Jesus.

Paul is discussing the life of faith and he is eager to show these believers how things work in them. The wonderful thing about being a child of God is that it is not a matter of achievement. It is not a matter of running the fastest mile or climbing the highest mountain. God through Christ Jesus makes the believer His child. This is what Paul is pointing out. "If Christ be in you" certain things will follow. The body is dead because of sin, but the Spirit is life because of righteousness.

To say "the body is dead because of sin" means that the flesh, the human body, the human nature, is in such condition that it is impossible to make any response to the will of God. The reason the natural body is unresponsive to the will of God is because sin has broken all the connections with God and there is no way for the Holy Spirit to get through.

But there is a condition which makes possible a response to God in and through the Holy Spirit, who is within the heart because this person is right with God. This righteousness is not the result of work and effort. The flesh is crucified and the Spirit is dwelling within. Man is crucified with Christ, and the Holy Spirit within him is responsive to the reality of God. Paul points out this situation in which the Christian lives, and then goes on to show a still more glorious result.

If the Spirit of Him that raised up Jesus from the dead dwells in the believer, this will bring the potential power of God into his very being—right into his soul. He that raised up Christ from the dead shall also quicken the mortal bodies of believers by His Spirit that dwells in them. In that sentence the significant word is "quicken," vitalized, made alive. When Paul refers to "mortal bodies" he means just what the words imply—bodies that are dying and will decay. Human bodies are like that, dead in trespasses and sin; and dying all the time men are living in them. These human bodies in themselves cannot respond to the will of God, but if any man has the Spirit of Him who raised up Jesus from the dead dwelling in him, his situation is different.

When Paul wrote that God would "quicken our mortal bodies by His Spirit," he was saying that our human capacities will become sensitive to the will of God. We do not have to do a thing about this. It is being done for us. All we can do is receive it. "But as many as received him, to them gave he power to become the sons of God." Our human nature is dead, but the Spirit is alive and if He is in us, He will give us life because of righteousness. We will be right in the sight of God and will be alive in the Spirit. We will let the Holy Spirit work in us.

Some may wonder what that will look like. If we become sensitive to the will of God, what difference will that make? Let us say that we get up in the morning and we have our family round about us. We could help to meet their needs with joy. We could prepare breakfast, serve it, help the children off to school, and do all this as unto God, rather than as a chore. If we have the Spirit of God in our hearts He will quicken our mortal bodies, i.e., make us sensitive to the will of God. Then serving others would become a pleasure because God would move us that way.

Consider traffic with all its rules and wild drivers. Having Christ Jesus in us will enable us to obey the rules with pleasure. We will be glad to do it. Yielding to others could be a pain in the neck, but with Christ in us our view is changed. It is a wonderful thing to have the desire in our hearts to do the right thing. We can be so affected by the grace of God and the Holy Spirit in our hearts that yielding to others can actually become a joy. Also, in this matter of forgiving a person who has done us wrong, would you believe that that can actually bring gladness to our hearts? These are some of the changes which take place in us when Christ is the hope of our glory, when the power that raised up Jesus Christ from the dead actually affects us so that we will be inclined to do the will of God.

8

The Spirit Enables People to Live

Romans 8:12-13

Did you know that the great blessing of being a Christian is that a believer can be delivered from his own human desires and his own human weaknesses?

One of the most pathetic sights that any of us ever see is that of an afflicted person who wants to move and cannot. He wants to act but he cannot do what he wants to do. I expect you have some friends like this, and I am mentioning it to you now with a real concern. Can you think of someone you know whose speech mechanism is partially paralyzed so that he cannot talk very plainly? Do you have any friends or perhaps members of your own family whose feet will not respond to their will? Perhaps you know someone whose fingers will not function. Just the other night I was with a friend who had hands he could not really close. You say, "Well, that is pathetic; why bring it up?" Because this is the spiritual condition of any man in his natural state. He just cannot do what should be done.

There are some people who are actually blind about God. They can walk out in the starlit night where the heavens declare the glory of God, but they fail to see that declaration. They look around and see things, and God's hand is all about them, but they do not feel that hand. They can read the Bible but it is just another book. They listen to the preacher but to them it is merely a message from a man. They are blind about God. There are some people, you know, who are deaf to the cry of the poor. Frankly, the poor are all around but these people just hate to see anyone who is poor. So far as they are concerned, if they never saw a poor man again, it would suit them just fine. Let the poor stay poor and die poor as far as they are concerned. They are deaf to the cry of the poor. There are people of whom it must be said that so far as doing what is right is concerned, they are lame. They cannot move. They know what ought to be done but they do not want to do it. There are people who cannot thank God. They are stunned. Their voices just will not work. They just cannot praise nor pray. This is the spiritual condition of anyone in his natural state.

This condition will vary with different people. They are not all crippled in the same way. But where their ego overshadows everything for instance, they are ambitious, but they never have enough; they are vain. What bothers them is that no one ever seems to appreciate them enough. They are sensitive. They have the feeling that everybody is against them all the time. They are irritable. Someone is always offending them. They may be selfish. There is never anything for anyone else. Everything they see is just for themselves.

The strange thing is that although these people spend all their time, their energy, and their thought in taking care of themselves, they are unhappy. They are distressed and they are miserable. They are oftentimes mean. They become ugly. They can be vindictive. They can even be malicious.

Some of you may wonder whether or not what is being said refers to some of your relatives or maybe some of the people in your own family. It should be recognized that these traits are not peculiar to any one person nor to any one family. Such a condition is to be found in the home, where people live. It is found in the office. It is found in traffic: you have seen them—people who cut in ahead of you, people who race on through and recklessly endanger other people's lives. Driving that way is ridiculous, of course, but some people are like that. Some people show these traits in school. Some are like that even in church. Wherever there are people, wherever there are human beings, this condition may be found.

Some people act as if they were paralyzed or lame. I could have told you that they were sinful. The cure is not in education and it is not in giving them higher wages. If you should give them higher wages, they would want still higher wages. The cure is not in better housing. It is not in better jobs. You have probably guessed it already. The whole truth is that so far as human beings are concerned, they must be born again. Human nature is just not good enough. When it is said they must be "born again," this does not mean such persons will get a second chance. Being "born again" means each will be a new creature.

Paul follows through in Romans chapter 8 to show how this happens. It is because of the indwelling Holy Spirit of God that there will be a change in conduct. Paul writes:

> Therefore, brethren, we are debtors, not to the flesh, to live after the flesh (Rom. 8:12).

When he says "debtors," he means under obligation. We do not have to live as human beings. We are not limited to that. We are not debtors to the flesh, to live after the flesh. We do not have to live in this world at this poor dying rate. We do not have to go the natural way.

> For if ye live after the flesh, ye shall die: but if ye through the Spirit do mortify the deeds of the body, ye shall live (Rom. 8:13).

In other words, if you live after the flesh you shall die. If you try to settle all matters in a human way you will just perish. It will not work.

The word *mortify* is not ordinarily used. In our common speech we seldom use it. We may sometimes speak about being "mortified" about someone's conduct, which means it nearly kills us. Someone may say, "That just killed me!" "That just slays me!" In former times a man might have said, "That mortifies me." All these expressions mean the same thing.

But the use of the word *mortify* in Paul's statement is more serious than that. "If ye through the Spirit do mortify the deeds of the body:" how would you "mortify" the deeds of the body? You must reckon yourself dead; then you shall live. This is possible since the Holy Spirit is in you when you are a believer. It is the believing people with the Holy Spirit within them who can mortify the deeds of the body. This truth was actually spelled out by Paul in his epistle to the Colossians, where he admonishes the believers to practice mortifying certain activities.

> Mortify therefore your members which are upon the earth; fornication, uncleanness, inordinate affection, evil concupiscence, and covetousness, which is idolatry (Col. 3:5).

Paul is saying here that the believer can mortify these things. So far as fornication is concerned, he can reckon himself to be dead. That will take care of it. Uncleanness could possibly mean pride, selfishness. To be unclean in the sight of God is to be selfish all the time. The way to be free from that is to count oneself dead.

This is what Paul was saying in Romans 8:13. "If ye through the Spirit do mortify the deeds of the body, ye shall live." How can this be done through the Spirit? We should remember the Spirit will show us the things of Christ. What is the big thing about Christ? He died on Calvary's cross. I am to deny myself and be crucified with Him. Just as surely as I deny myself so that I am crucified with Him, I do not care about natural things. I get a little relief after something happens to me that is really upsetting me when someone says to me, "Fifty years from now it won't matter." That is the truth; likewise a hundred years from now it will matter less. When I am dead, it will be long gone. Perhaps you feel such procedure is a trick. By all means go ahead and use it. It is a good trick. It is a good way to deal with yourself, and the Holy Spirit can fix it so that it is not exactly a trick, because you can be crucified with Christ; yet you will live "if you will mortify the deeds of the body." Just as surely as you reckon yourself dead, the Lord will raise you up. So in every part of life, reckon yourself dead. In any quarrel you need to reckon yourself dead, because a dead man does not quarrel. You can be assured the Lord will raise you up. A dead man does not care where the neighbor parks his car. But the Lord will raise him up. You need to follow this on through. This is spiritual truth and it is for you. The Lord wants you to have it. It is the blessing of the Holy Spirit of God who will take the things of Christ and show them unto you and give you the victory in Him.

9

The Spirit Leads Believers into Sonship

Romans 8:14-15

The truth of the leading of the Holy Spirit deals largely with the Christian life and experience, but I am glad to set it forth for everybody. I am hoping that readers will get enough understanding to see something of the great privilege that belongs to the believer. Perhaps someone may not want to be moved blindly to turn to the Lord. He might like to come to the Lord with his eyes open. I can understand that very, very well, and I hope that as one reads, he will open his eyes and will look at these things of Christian experience as Paul sets them out when he writes:

For as many as are led by the Spirit of God, they are the sons of God (Rom. 8:14).

This statement does not mean that the Spirit of God leads men into the relationship of being sons of God. It is not saying the Spirit came upon them as human beings and so affected them as to guide and direct them in such a way that they finally achieved the status of sons. This sentence does not say that as many as are led by the Spirit of God become the sons of God. The Spirit of God would not have been leading them if they had not been sons. Actually what it means is to say that when anyone is being led by the Spirit of God, this is the evidence that that person is now a son of God. We must be careful to keep things in their proper order. By receiving Jesus Christ as my Savior and Lord, I am accepted in Him. Then because I am now accepted as a son, God send the Spirit of His Son into my heart that I may have the blessed benefit of His leading.

When I say that I am accepted in Him, I mean that I, as a believer, become identified with Jesus Christ as my Savior. He is the only begotten Son of God, but when I become identified with Him, I am born again into the family of God, and I become adopted as a son of God myself. Because I am now accepted as a son, adopted as a son, God sends forth the Spirit of His Son into my heart (Gal. 4:6).

When the Spirit of God comes into my heart, He takes charge. The flesh, the human nature, is reckoned as dead. The Spirit now lifts me and leads me into His will. When the Spirit leads me, there is no need to think I am unwilling. The Spirit will not start functioning in me until I have received Christ Jesus as my Savior. If I have received Christ Jesus as my Savior, I have yielded myself to Him. I have denied myself. I have reckoned myself dead, so to speak. "I am crucified with Christ: nevertheless I live . . . and the life which I now live in the flesh I live by the faith of the Son of God, who loved me, and gave himself for me" (Gal. 2:20).

Being led by the Spirit of God can be a joyous, glad, willing service of love. Someone may say, "No one ever wants to do anything for God's sake." But this is not true. Have you ever had anyone in love with you? Perhaps a little child was in love with you, and you can remember how that child wanted to do things for you. When a little child loves his mother, he is eager to do things for her. How often he gets in the way trying to do things for her! It is a joyous, glad, willing service of love on the part of the child. When we think of believers who are led by the Spirit of God, we should not think of them as being surly and sulky, as if they were being led against their will. We may think of them as being glad, joyous, willing, ready to serve. They are the sons of God.

> For ye have not received the spirit of bondage again to fear; but ye have received the Spirit of adoption, whereby we cry, Abba, Father (Rom. 8:15).

The motivation for living as a believer in Christ is never a matter of compulsion. The believer is not compelled to do certain things. Before I was a believer, if I ever thought of God, I thought of facing the Judge. The idea of doing anything in God's sight was a matter of doing it for the Judge, who would judge me if I failed to do it right. That is how it will be when the natural man faces his Judge, but that is not the way it is with a Christian.

The natural man at his best feels guilty before God in his sin. Every now and then I meet people in church who seem to feel that way. Then I try to tell them, just as nicely as I know how, that it would be a whole lot different if they accepted Jesus Christ as their Savior. You show me a person who is depressed because he feels that he is such a sinner: what he feels is true enough, but he does not have to stay in that condition. Even if it is true that he is that big a sinner, he needs to hear and believe "though your sins be as scarlet, they shall be as white as snow; though they be red like crimson, they shall be as wool" (Isa. 1:18).

This promise is what he needs to believe, because when he once believes that Christ Jesus died for him, his conscience will be purged from dead works so he can serve the living God. A believing person will be freed. Suppose someone says, "But, you did wrong." That is the truth: he did wrong. And this is no small thing. But Christ Jesus died for him. Sin is terrible. It put Christ on the cross. God raised Christ from the dead and now He would have the believing sinner rejoice in Him. The believer has settled all that was against him by turning to the Lord.

When John was writing his epistle, he wrote:

My little children, these things write I unto you, that ye sin not. And if any man sin, we have an advocate with the Father, Jesus Christ the righteous (I John 2:1).

I wish the whole wide world understood that those of us who are believers are forgiven, and that we are forgiven for Christ's sake and not because we are good. We are forgiven because He is gracious. Anyone can have forgiveness. God is no respecter of persons. There is not a single thing in anyone's life that He could not forgive. The mind and the heart of man cannot think up a sin so dark that the blood of the Lord Jesus Christ could not cleanse him and this He will do. When He has done this for the sinner, the forgiven soul will be glad to serve Him in any way he can. The believer has been forgiven everything that was against him; and the blood of Christ Jesus has cleansed the believer so that he might serve the living and true God (Heb. 9:14). And now, coming to the Father in His beloved Son there is no cloud of fear. You have not received the spirit of bondage again to fear; you have received the Spirit of adoption (Rom. 8:15). You are included in the family so that your heart will cry, "Abba, Father."

The word "Abba" is what is called a diminutive. The word *Daddy* is the diminutive of *Dad*. In similar fashion the word *Mommy* is the diminutive of *Mom*. It is the same with the word *Babe* and the diminutive *baby*. It is even so with *Tom* and *Tommy* and *Bill* and *Billy*. In the Hebrew language the word for Father is *Ab*. Thus, *Abba* is just like *Daddy*. I have taken the time to bring this to your mind because what Paul is saying is that the Spirit of the Son, the Spirit of the Lord Jesus Christ, the Holy Spirit of God, in the heart of the believer will cause him to look up into the face of Almighty God, as a little girl would look up into the face of her father, whom she loves and calls by her special name, Daddy. The Holy Spirit enables the believer to nestle into the arms of God. Any man who will let that happen to him will be a better man than he ever was before. That experience of fellowship with God as Father will permanently affect the believer. "The goodness of God leadeth thee to repentance" (Rom. 2:4).

10

The Holy Spirit Gives Assurance

Romans 8:16

Could you understand how a person might be uncertain about his being a child of God?

The Spirit itself beareth witness with our spirit, that we are the children of God (Rom. 8:16).

The whole matter of the believer belonging to God as a member of His household is hard to accept as truth. No matter how often you hear it said, nor how many times you sing the hymns, it is difficult for the human heart to believe that a person who was a sinner really does belong to God.

Yet it is very important that the believer be assured of this relationship. The believer is blessed in Christ Jesus, and the word *blessed* means he is to be strong in joy and in gladness and in peace. To say the believer is blessed in Christ Jesus is to say he is to have his eternal life in Christ Jesus; he is to have joy and satisfaction in Christ Jesus; and he is to have peace and comfort in Christ Jesus. Scripture says, "The joy of the Lord shall be your strength." Believers generally do not sympathize with one who is uncertain about his belonging to the family of God. It seems easier to sympathize with one who has difficulty in believing God is invisible. A person can walk out into his yard and see the yard, the street, the cars, and the people. But when he looks up into the sky, the trees, the birds, he does not see God. God is invisible, and yet the believer's faith is in Him. For spiritual experience faith is necessary.

It is normal to think about the future. If someone should die, at his funeral the preacher is expected to talk about heaven. It is probable that, generally speaking, believers in Christ believe in heaven. But will believers take that faith out in daylight? Will they take it down to the office with them? Will they take it with them in their car? Do believers really and truly believe these promises that they belong to God and that God belongs to them?

It is easy enough to realize, of course, that believers cannot leave Him in their church. It is not a case that true believers go to church because they want to meet God and that when they come away from church they leave God behind them. That would be an unworthy idea of God. And we can be sure that will not happen. If the believer knows God at all, He will be in the believer's home just as He would be in the church during the service. God will be right there in the office, or in the shop. He will be right there on the farm. He will be right there wherever the believer is; God is everywhere. But to believe that, to get that into the consciousness, is not easy. It is written "it doth not yet appear what we shall be" (I John 3:2). Believers need assurance about this. There is no one living here on earth who has ever been to heaven and can tell believers what it is going to be like.

Some believers, so far as living is concerned, have troubles. "Now for a season, if need be, ye are in heaviness through manifold temptations" (I Peter 1:6). When a believer has real trouble, I mean crying trouble, weeping trouble, heart-sickening trouble, he needs to be kept by the power of God through faith. It is not an easy thing for a believer to keep in mind and heart that he really does belong to God. It would be very easy to lose his joy when he loses his assurance and confidence. This tendency emphasizes the real importance of this text: "The Spirit itself beareth witness with our spirit, that we are the children of God" (Rom. 8:16). It is obvious God wants the believer to know with joy that he really does belong. It might be helpful if every believing person would walk into every room in his house, and standing there, say to himself, "God is here with me." Let the woman go into her kitchen and say, "God is here with me." Let the man go down into the basement and say, "God is here with me." Let any believer go up to his bedroom and say, "God is here with me." Let him go out to his garage and say, "God is here with me." Any believer could go down to his office, and sitting at his desk, ask himself, "Am I a believer? Is God here?" If He is anywhere, He is there.

God has arranged for the believer. He has given him His Holy Spirit, and "the Spirit itself beareth witness with our spirit, that we are the children of God." No matter how the believer does, no matter how poorly he does, and no matter how little he understands, no matter how limited he may be, there comes up from the inside of his heart when he is a believer in the Lord Jesus Christ the assurance that he belongs to Christ. It will come to him that Christ Jesus died for the ungodly, and since he is one of the ungodly, then Christ died for him and his heart at once is comforted. He will remember "whosoever cometh to me shall in no wise be cast out." And he comes. So he has the promise of God: he will not be cast out. Christ Jesus rose from the dead on his behalf and Christ is alive now remembering him. Christ is interceding on his behalf right now in the presence of God. That is really true. The believer reads in Scripture and deep down in his believing heart he has the certain assurance: Christ is coming again. The believer will see Him. Christ is coming to receive him to Himself.

The Holy Spirit is given to the believer to keep bringing these things to his mind. While the believer is in this world, he will never get to the top of some high mountain to get a peek into heaven. It won't happen that way. He will read it in the Bible. The promise will be there before him. How can he get the assurance of it? "The Spirit itself bears witness with our spirit, that we are the children of God." It will not do the believer any harm to pray. If he will take time for prayer, the Holy Spirit can speak to him. Nor will it do any harm for him to go to church regularly, especially to a church where the gospel is preached. The believer could find some place where the man who reads the Bible believes it. Believing people ought to be in church from time to time. They ought to read their Bibles from time to time. They ought to pray from time to time. What will happen when they do? The Holy Spirit Himself will bear witness with their spirits that they are the children of God.

Even the disciples themselves as they followed the Lord Jesus found that on occasion their faith would falter. Believers are after all only human beings and they cannot keep their faith strong in their own strength. Faith needs to be grounded in certain events and promises of God. John in his first epistle outlines the truth that can help believers to know that they have eternal life.

> These things have I written unto you that believe on the name of the Son of God; that ye may know that ye have eternal life, and that ye may believe on the name of the Son of God (I John 5:13).

There are certain ways in which a believer can know that he belongs: if he believes that Jesus is the Son of God and if he loves the brethren. He does not have to make up his mind to love the brethren. He will be moved to do this when he looks into the face of Jesus Christ and sees what God has done for him in Christ Jesus. It will come to him, and just as surely as he cares about other people, just as surely as he cares about missions, just as surely as he cares about doing work among the poor, just as surely as he cares about winning souls to Christ, he will have the evidence that he really does belong.

If he has the Holy Spirit in his heart, which of course he has when he believes in Christ and puts his trust in Him; and if he is conscious of that, he will be assured that he belongs to Christ. If he would get answers to prayer, if praying mattered in his life, he could add up all these evidences and they would help him to know that he has eternal life. It is not just a matter of logical argument, but the Holy Spirit will use these things and bring them to you. I can remember my own case. As a young man I was an agnostic. I did not believe there was a God until after I was out teaching school. But then while I was a young man I came to believe in the reality of God. And soon I came to believe in the Lord Jesus Christ, which led to a marvelous experience of conversion. Yet several years after that came a time when I doubted that I really belonged. I felt that I was sinful and I was in a terrible state of depression. Then I spent one whole day out in the woods up in Canada. It was a day in spring. I had my Bible and I stayed alone, sitting on a stump from nine in the morning until four in the afternoon. I read and I prayed and I read and I prayed, and then it came to me.

> Whosoever therefore shall confess me before men, him will I confess also before my Father which is in heaven (Matt. 10:32).

I had confessed Him before men, and so He would confess me before His Father. You might say, "You just read that in the Bible." But it was more than just reading it. Certainly I had read it and I had reread it. But the Spirit Himself bore witness with my spirit that I really did belong to God. So I would say if you are in any doubt, take time to seek His face. Let Him show Himself to you. The Holy Spirit will help you to believe the promises of God.

11

Glory Awaits the Spirit-led Believers

Romans 8:17-18

Did you know that suffering is involved in Christian growth and life? Throughout this discussion the interest has been in the life and the welfare of believers. It is possible that even believers themselves do not always understand what is involved in the gospel. One reason why Paul wrote his letters might be so that he could explain the gospel more fully. It is so easy for people to feel that they know what a believer is, what he should do, and then they set the rules by which the believer should live. John says one reason the world does not know the believers is that unbelievers do not know Christ, and

Paul agrees. Paul says very plainly that if they had known the truth about Christ, they never would have crucified Him, but they did! To understand the gospel we cannot go by popular opinion. To know the truth of the Christian life we must go by the Bible.

It should always be remembered that a believer is not some special kind of human being. He is not someone who is so very good or so very strong, nor so very kind, nor so very meek, nor so very loving. Such characteristics do not necessarily make a believer. Every person was born as a human being. Every true believer is born again as a child of God.

This matter of being born again is not always a simple matter to understand. In one way it can be stated as an easy experience, and there are men who preach it that way. Sometimes we hear evangelists talking about what a simple thing it is to accept Christ. I can remember some years ago shortly after I became a Christian, I heard a man talking that way and emphasizing what a simple thing it was to become a Christian. I listened to him and I knew that in one sense what he was saying was true, and yet in some way or other it did not seem to fit right. When he told us in his talk that it was just as easy as taking off a coat or putting on a coat, or walking through a door or opening a door, somehow this did not seem to be an adequate explanation. As I got to thinking more and more about it, I finally realized how simple and how profound it is. Becoming a Christian is just as simple as dying.

Actually, dying is very simple. A person can do that when he cannot do anything else. There is not anyone in the world who cannot die. Little babies, old men, young, strong, or weak men, anyone can die. But dying is a very profound thing. Its simplicity does not make dying cheap. This is the way it is with being a Christian. A person can believe in the Lord Jesus Christ and accept Him, and there is a sense in which that is as easy as shutting the door. Have you ever seen a man die? It is a very simple thing. You would be surprised how easy it is for a person to die. And yet how profound! So it is with being a Christian.

The matter of becoming a Christian involves several simple things. There is first of all the dying: "If any man will be my disciple, let him deny himself." Then there is the aspect of being buried. I do not think many people realize that. My own daughter helped me to see it better than anything I have ever seen. I remember one time talking to her about how important it was to realize that becoming a believer is like dying, and then it is like being raised from the dead. And she stopped me. She said, "Daddy, there is something in between. After you die, when you die to self, you go into a state when you just do not know anything and you just cannot feel anything." She had been through it. Then I knew what being in the "grave" is like.

The Lord Jesus was three days in the grave. It is not only a matter of letting go and dying, in that sense, but when a person really lets go, he is altogether undone, buried, then raised from the dead in the resurrection. But that is not all! When our Lord Jesus Christ was raised from the dead, He did not stay here. He went where He is now. He went into the very presence of God.

Thus the course of becoming a believer involves dying, being buried, being raised, and communing with God.

> And if children, then heirs; heirs of God, and joint-heirs with Christ; if so be that we suffer with him, that we may be also glorified together. For I reckon that the sufferings of this present time are not worthy to be compared with the glory which shall be revealed in us (Rom. 8:17-18).

Note in these verses how suffering and being glorified go together; and they go an that order: first suffering, then being glorified. That is like death and life, death and resurrection. We know that death and resurrection go together. Resurrection cannot take place if there has not been death. Glory cannot come if there has not been suffering. Thus dying, the way a person starts the life of believing in Christ, is not always easy. It can involve suffering.

Our Lord Jesus Christ was crucified, that is true! He was crucified on Calvary, as we know. But He was in agony before Calvary. Gethsemane came first, involving deep suffering, then came Calvary. How much Jesus of Nazareth endured in suffering in His lifetime is not written. We do know that it says about Him, "He was a man of sorrows, and acquainted with grief." If a believer should be suffering, he should keep it in mind that suffering this could be related to a glory that is to come to him. There is one thing for sure, as certainly as a believer puts his trust in the Lord Jesus Christ, his suffering will not be in vain. So when a believer suffers, he can take courage.

Christ Jesus suffered unto death, and the servant is not greater than his Master. The Word of God promises that if we suffer with Him, we will be also glorified together.

> For I reckon that the sufferings of this present time are not worthy to be compared with the glory which shall be revealed in us (Rom. 8:18).

We will be the children of God, seated with Him, sharing His glory. Believers can always be strengthened by remembering the fact that suffering can actually lead to glory.

12

All Creation Awaits Deliverance by the Spirit

Romans 8:19-25

Have you ever felt that the whole world is waiting for something better than has ever happened? Death is the one common dread of the world, just as it is the one sure event that awaits every living thing. I often feel when I am preaching about death that there is one thing I would like to tell everybody: I didn't make this world, I didn't plan it. I am not responsible for the fact that every flower is going to wilt, that every blade of grass will wither, that every person will die. Death is not my fault, if you want to put it that way. People everywhere have been concerned about death. Throughout the ages of history and culture, men have been both fascinated and horrified by death.

Every great poet has at least one poem dealing with death. The average man has one impression about death. It might be that dying wouldn't be so bad, but it is just so permanent; and death looms so inevitable. Living things try to avoid death. Animals fear death. Our loved ones dread death. So often death brings regret and sadness. It is against this background that you and I need to realize plainly that the Christian gospel is the one shining exception to this widespread dread of death.

Christ Jesus rose from the dead. One thing believers can tell the world: death has lost its sting and the grave has lost its victory. When Jesus of Nazareth was teaching, there were people who asked Him to give them a sign, a symbol of His message; and He told them the only sign He would ever give them was the sign of the prophet Jonah. In that context He told them that He would be raised from the dead after three days in the bowels of the earth.

The full meaning of death often escapes general attention, as well as the full meaning of the common longing for life. Everyone wants to avoid death: the fear of death is all over; but in the Bible that fear is removed. Romans 8:19-25 are some of the most difficult verses Paul has written. As we go slowly verse by verse through this passage we will see the relationship it has to the truth of the Holy Spirit. In verse 18 Paul states that the sufferings of this present time are not worthy to be compared with the glory which shall follow in the case of the believer. Then Paul goes on to say in verse 19, "For the earnest expectation of the creature waiteth for the manifestation of the sons of God." It will be helpful to replace the word *creature* with the word *creation*. When Paul used the word *creature* he did not mean to imply some animal. He meant a living thing, a created thing. This would now read "the earnest expectation of the creation waiteth for the manifestation of the sons of God." In these words Paul is referring to the general truth, mentioned elsewhere in Scripture, that this whole world is dominated by the fear of death. At the same time all creation longs for the daylight, the brilliance of the freedom of the resurrection, "the manifestation of the sons of God." Following verse 18, where it was stated that sufferings were to be ignored by the believer because the glory that was to come was appreciated, there is this statement about the deep earnest expectation in the created world. "The whole world" is waiting for the day when death will be gone. That is the promise of the Bible.

"For the creature was made subject to vanity, not willingly, but by reason of him who hath subjected the same in hope" (Rom. 8:20). By using again the word *creation* the statement now reads, "the creation was made subject to vanity, not willingly, but by reason of him who hath subjected the same in hope." This seems to imply that the whole creation is suffering, as it were, in subjection to this uselessness, the futility of living. If in the last analysis all one is going to do is die, then it is not worth much to live. If everything that you can gather you've got to leave here, why gather it? Such thoughts are discouraging. The whole of creation is in the same situation. Why grow beautiful flowers when all they are going to do is wilt? Why have these lovely roses when all they are going to do is die? Why see these beautiful birds and hear them sing when every one of them is going to die?

The sentence of death is upon the whole world, and don't think for one moment that anyone is happy about it. Birds don't like it, animals don't like it, men don't like it, mothers don't like it, children don't like it, friends don't like it, loved ones don't like it, sweethearts don't like it. Nobody likes it. In fact, everybody is against it. And this is true all over the world. Now the creation, the creature "was made subject to" this futility, this "vanity," this emptiness of living, "not willingly." The creatures did not agree to it. They didn't want it. It was imposed upon them by God: "but by reason of him who hath subjected the same in hope."

But God never intended that death was to be the end of everything. For this reason He sent His Son, because His Son was raised from the dead. It is written, "He took not on him the nature of angels" (Heb. 2:16), because if He had, He wouldn't have had to die. He took on Him the nature of Abraham "that He might taste death" and set those free who all their lifetime are subject to bondage because of the fear of death. That is what Jesus Christ came into the world for, and He seems to have opened the way for all creation. "Because the creature (the creation) itself also shall be delivered from the bondage of corruption into the glorious liberty of the children of God" (Rom. 8:21). This great promise seems to imply that the whole created world is going to be set free from death. How could anyone believe that? Because Christ Jesus rose from the dead: that is how it can be believed.

Since the body of Jesus Christ was raised from the dead, "the whole creation itself shall be delivered from the bondage of corruption." It will be set free from death and decay "into the glorious liberty of the children of God"—the liberty in glory of the children of God. This seems to be the case at all levels of creation. "For we know that the whole creation groaneth and travaileth in pain together until now" (Rom. 8:22). The creation is suffering while waiting. Animals, human beings, social groups, domestic situations in homes groan and travail in pain. In this world there is much trouble and suffering and worry and distress, and all wish to God they were out of it.

"And not only they, but ourselves also, which have the firstfruits of the Spirit" (Rom. 8:23). Believers already have the first fruits of the new life, because when they received the Holy Spirit of God they received something that will never die. The one element in believers that will never die is in the Holy Spirit of God, who was given to them now and will be with them in heaven, always and forever. Believers have the firstfruits of the Spirit, but they long for the resurrection. Paul writes about this: we "groan within ourselves, waiting for the adoption, to wit, the redemption of our body." Sometimes believers groan because of sickness, sometimes they groan because of their own limitations, or because of other people's meanness, or because of varied distresses. Believers all groan waiting for the redemption of the body.

45

And so believers are looking forward to something. Thus Paul could write, "For we are saved by hope (confident expectation of something that has been promised): but hope that is seen is not hope: for what a man seeth, why doth he yet hope for? But if we hope for that we see not, then do we with patience wait for it" (Rom. 8:24-25). Scripture holds out the expectation there is a bright day coming by and by. That is the glorious promise of the Bible. There are better days ahead. It is dark now, but it will be daylight later. The believer's future is guaranteed. It is not here yet, but it is coming. Every believing person lives and dies and is buried with the confident expectation of the resurrection of the dead. Believers are going on through to glory. Praise God!

13

The Spirit Helps in Praying

Romans 8:26-27

Have you ever realized that praying people need help to know what to pray for? "For we know not what we should pray for as we ought" (Rom. 8:26). This verse brings to mind something everybody is conscious of one way or another: men do not know what to pray for. I am conscious of the fact that not all who read this pray, or at least pray as they ought. Perhaps you are not against praying; you may be just not certain what difference praying makes. I am confident if you knew what actually would happen in answer to prayer, you would pray unceasingly. But how to pray and what to pray for is still the problem.

Consider what happens when sick people come to see the doctor. Some of the sick come to the doctor and try to tell him what is wrong with them and what he should prescribe. I expect every doctor knows about that. And that is the way some people pray. They are coming to talk to God, and feel they must tell God what to do. Some even have the idea that if they cannot be specific in their request as to exactly what they want, they should not bother the Lord. This idea suggests they believe that the Lord will not have any ideas of His own. The truth is that men do not know what to pray for as they ought. But still men should pray.

The great promises that encourage praying for anything, that encourage praying for whatever is on the heart, usually include the phrase "in thy name." "If you shall ask anything in my name, I will do it." That phrase "in my name" implies a desire to receive whatever is in His will. Even so, though we may admit that we do not always know what He wants, and we do not always know what the will of God would be, we should be all means be constant in praying, because praying is not a matter of telling God what to do, but it is a matter of asking God to do what He has in mind to do. We should be ready to give Him the praise and the glory.

Paul sets out a wonderful encouragement when he tells us how the Holy Spirit will help.

> Likewise the Spirit also helpeth our infirmities: for we know not what we should pray for as we ought: but the Spirit itself maketh intercession for us with groanings which cannot be uttered. And he that searcheth the hearts knoweth what is the mind of the Spirit, because he maketh intercession for the saints according to the will of God (Rom. 8:26-27).

These verses should be read together because they tell the whole story. "The Spirit also helpeth our infirmities": our understanding, our infirmities are our weaknesses. We are weak oftentimes in our understanding, and we are weak in appreciating His will. Many times we really do not know what God wants: we are just weak about it; and sometimes even when we have an idea of what may be in the will of God, we are too weak to ask for it.

Who would ever be strong enough to ask for illness in his family? Who would actually ask God to bring sickness? Believers know that many times sickness is a blessing, and that some members of the family actually can be brought nearer to God because they have been stricken down in a major illness. But who would have enough strength, who would be able to ask God to send sickness? or to send an accident? I wonder what wife would pray God to send an accident to her husband. Yet in some cases, such an accident could be very meaningful. Or who would ask God to send death?

Believers are not strong enough and they are not wise enough to ask for the best God can do. That is part of the infirmity. But "the Spirit . . . helpeth our infirmities." When believers pray, they exercise themselves according to their understanding, and they speak out of their minds. But in praying, in addition to words, there can be an urgency, there can be a yearning, that would be expressed in a groaning. The believer can be asking God for help and he may have in mind that it is very very important that God should act. Perhaps he has a child going to school, and he asks God that his child should be blessed in school. So in prayer he cries out, "Oh, Lord, bless my boy." These were the expressed words, but the groaning in his heart was more than words. In a sense the groaning is actually unexpressed words.

"But the Spirit itself maketh intercession for us with groanings which cannot be uttered" (Rom. 8:26). My words in praying could well be, "Oh, God, bless my daughter, mmm." Now when I say "bless my daughter," I may be thinking of her children; but when I groan and I put this "mmm," the Holy Spirit is calling on God to do for this girl of mine what I don't even know; but the Holy Spirit knows. God knows, and when He hears the groanings of the Spirit, He knows what is being asked for; and He will do that. When a believer prays, there is always another One praying with him, the Holy Spirit, and God hears the Spirit.

I want to share an incident with you. A country preacher told of his needing a new suit. He told how he went on his knees to God in prayer, saying: "Lord, I think this suit is too shabby for preaching. Now, I think if I could have a new suit it would look better, and it would be more fitting for the message I give, and I wish that you would just arrange that I would get a new suit." Then he went on to tell: "I was praying this way and while I was on my knees praying like that, the Holy Spirit was talking to the Father. The Father heard the Holy Spirit. I didn't hear Him. I don't know what He said. It's very possible that the Holy Spirit was saying to the Father, 'Father, don't pay any attention to him. The suit he's got now is good enough, and if he gets a new suit, he will just be proud. The way he is now, humble in that old suit, his preaching actually has power. If he was to get all dressed up, he might lose his power, so Father, don't give it to him.' While I was asking God for a new suit, the Holy Spirit was already saying to the Father, 'Father, do better than that for him. Just don't give him one right now. It wouldn't be good for him.' And so I didn't get the suit."

When you as a believer pray for anything at all, whatever it may be, you should remember that God already knows you. He already has you in mind. There is not a possible situation that you can bring before Him that Almighty God does not know about, and that He does not care about. Someone might say, "In that case I don't need to pray." And I would at once gently tell you, "Hush your mouth! God wants you to pray." Why should you pray even when you ask for the wrong things? Because your asking Him enables Him to do in response to your request for the glory of the name of the Lord Jesus Christ. When a believer prays to God, he does not twist God's arm to get God to do something He did not want to do. Praying is not aiming to get God to change His mind and to do differently from what He had in mind to do. Praying is reaching out to receive from Him what He was going to do. A believer can do more when he prays than he can do when he does not pray. So a believer should be "instant in prayer" all day long and all night long, wherever he goes and about everything. If a believer will pray, God can do things for him which will be beyond his understanding. The Holy Spirit will pray with him.

14

The Operation of the Spirit
Activates Righteousness

Philippians 2:13

Have you ever considered that when a believer does right, he does not deserve all the credit for such conduct? "For it is God which worketh in you both to will and to do of his good pleasure" (Phil. 2:13). When Paul was telling the Philippians to work out their own salvation, they were to remember this truth. There are so many different ways a person can act and can be and can do. Some of them are good, some of them are bad. Actually as far as our conduct is concerned we are already set up for the way in which we are going to act and live. A person may not be able to predict when a frog is going to jump, nor how far he is going to jump. But anyone can tell in which direction he is going to jump. He is going to jump straight ahead in the way he is pointed. So it is with people. Everyone is already pointed to go in a certain direction. He will go straight ahead as he is pointed at the present time, based upon his background, wants, and direction. Most persons have some point of view, some direction or goal, and certain resources by which they will undertake to achieve. This is true of all people everywhere.

A believer has most of his life settled. He belongs to God. He has been bought with a price. He has been reconciled to God. He is adopted as a child of God, and he is in constant communion with God by the Holy Spirit. When he accepts Jesus Christ as his Savior, his goal is set. The believer will be with Christ. This is something he didn't fight for, work for, or buy. God called him. The believer came and was received because he has been bought with a price: the blood of the Lord Jesus Christ. He has been reconciled to God by the death of the Lord Jesus Christ. He has been adopted as a child by the grace of God, and he is in constant communion with God through the Holy Spirit.

Because all this is true, a believer is not his own. He has denied himself, he reckons himself dead, he has yielded himself to the Lord, and he has received the Holy Spirit of God. The Holy Spirit keeps reminding him of the things of Jesus Christ. The Christian's direction and goal is already settled. Anyone who believes in the Lord Jesus Christ and has accepted Him has one aim: he is ambitious to be well-pleasing to God. This has been verified in my personal experience. I can tell the whole wide world with a clear conscience, as God is my witness, that if I could do it, I would want to be well-pleasing in His sight. There is no organization, no institution, no group of people, there is nothing on earth as important to my poor soul as the pleasure of my Lord and Savior Jesus Christ who died for me. And that is not because I am good; but because God laid His hands on me. Now I have that aim.

The same is true in the matter of walking in the Spirit. The believer will be reverent toward God. He will serve the Lord with gladness. He would like to see God's name glorified. You could not hurt the believer more than by ignoring his God. And when people criticize God, they are criticizing the believer's best friend. The believer makes it a point whenever the name of God is spoken to bow his heart. He goes to church and to prayer meeting. He will go anywhere he can in order to mingle with other believers who praise the Lord God. He will do all this because he honors and worships God. These considerations that the Holy Spirit brings to the believer's mind are dynamic: they move him to action. This is the plan of God for all the saved ones.

15

Deliverance from Carnal Thinking
Is by the Spirit

II Corinthians 5:17

Have you any idea how a believer is delivered from old evil habits? "Therefore if any man be in Christ, he is a new creature: old things are passed away; behold, all things are become new" (II Cor. 5:17). This is how Paul described the believer. "If any man be in Christ" means *anybody:* "whosoever will may come." And when a man accepts Christ, he is a new creature, a new creation. It isn't just a matter of starting over again; he is different. "Old things are passed away; behold, all things are become new." This is the wonderful blessing in being a believer: each day is a new day. It seems that believers themselves often fail to appreciate this fully, but it is true. A believer can start each day forgetting the things that are behind. That is absolutely true for every believer because Christ Jesus carries away his sins: He bears the burden.

Paul writes about himself:

Among whom also we all had our conversation in times past in the lusts of our flesh, fulfilling the desires of the flesh and of the mind (Eph. 2:3).

The apostle himself had lived a natural worldly life before he became a believer. When he became a believer, he was a new creation. Peter also writes this way:

For the time past of our life may suffice us to have wrought the will of the Gentiles, when we walked in lasciviousness, lusts, excess of wine, revellings, banquetings, and abominable idolatries (I Peter 4:3).

In this way Peter described the early part of his life before he became a believer. When he accepted Christ, he became a new creation.

The evil habits of the natural person, however, are not always vulgar or indecent. They are not always ugly. Actually pride can be civilized. A person can be proud in many decent ways, but it is still evil. "God resisteth the proud." Vanity can be so sweet. One can see delicate people, really sweet persons, who are vain and empty-headed. Selfishness can be highly educated, sophisticated, and yet as evil as the devil. Being uncharitable is an evil thing. Ignoring the poor can be done by people who live in fine homes, dress in silks and satins and furs and feathers. Such things can happen. Nice persons can be cruel and envious. A woman can be sweet and yet be envious of some other woman. In her own heart she can feel just like a cat so far as the other woman is concerned—she would scratch her if she could. But she can keep all this covered if she has been well trained and has been brought up in a nice home. A person can be covetous so that he looks at other people with an eye that is green with envy and jealousy, and yet that person can be civilized and moral and cultured. But we can thank God that a person can be delivered from all of these things.

There are several catalogs of carnal, sinful activities set forth in the Bible. Paul writes in Romans 1:29-32, "Being filled with all unrighteousness," and then he goes on and tells what that includes. In Galatians 5:19-21 Paul writes, "Now the works of the flesh are manifest," and then describes them, and when the list is finished he adds "and such like." If he didn't happen to name any particular sin, he meant to include it too. In Colossians 3:5-8 he writes, "Mortify therefore your members which are upon the earth . . . put off all these [activities that are evil]." In II Timothy 3:1-9 he writes, "Perilous times shall come. For men shall be lovers of their own selves" and then follows with a list of evil actions, winding up by saying, "their folly shall be manifest unto all men."

It is easy to miss the message of Scripture in which God shows that evil is evil and will not be acceptable to Him, that He is of purer eyes than to behold evil. Wherever there is sin of any sort, believers need to repudiate it and confess it to God. Every person is born in sin and grows up in it. There is not a single person that isn't contaminated with sin. Sin is the easier seen when it is dirty, and when it is crude and vulgar. It as hard to recognize when it is civilized and refined and educated and perfumed, but it is sin all the time.

Is it possible ever to be free from such things? Can a believer be free from the influence of the past? Can he be free from the memory of these things? There is the story of Naaman the Syrian, a great military captain who was a leper. He went to Elisha for help. He was told to go to the River Jordan and wash, that he might be healed. As the story unfolds it tells how he went and washed, and his leprosy was cleansed. Then comes this remarkable sentence: "his flesh came again as the flesh of a little child." That meant no scars. Just so the believer can be delivered from all the evil.

The actual deliverance of a believer is by way of Calvary. All the evil in him is in the flesh, in his human nature. He can take that to the cross and let it die. Then by faith he is buried. When he is raised from the dead, it is not the old man that is raised. It is not the flesh that is raised. It is the new man, "in the newness of life."

The practical deliverance that occurs in believers is through the Holy Spirit of God. The Holy Spirit reminds the believer of the death of the Lord Jesus Christ for him, and prompts him to believe in Christ and commit himself to Christ and be baptized into His death. He is to deny himself, take up his cross, and follow Christ. The Holy Spirit does this when He reminds the believer that the thing to do with the old man is to let him die. The believer's natural sinfulness will now be in the grave with Christ. Then the Holy Spirit will help the believer to surrender, to let go of himself. In that way he can be freed from envy. When he lets go of himself, he can be freed from malice. That is the way to be freed from appetite, from lust, from desire. The believer needs to let go and surrender so far as he is concerned in himself. The Holy Spirit enables the believer to respond to the Father in the newness of life, in the resurrection. So far as the believer is concerned, the evil that used to be in his whole personality and in his life is not so much controlled as it is forgotten.

It is first forgiven, and then forgotten. The evil is not so much condemned as it is ignored. The believer turns away from it. He need not do anything with it, but leave it in the grave. He is to die unto self and be raised in Christ, free in Him. The Holy Spirit will remind him of this and that will help to set him free in his habits and his conduct.

16

The Spirit Knows the Deep Things of God

I Corinthians 2:10

Can you understand that no human being can ever discover what is in the mind of God?

But God hath revealed them unto us by his Spirit: for the Spirit searcheth all things, yea, the deep things of God (I Cor. 2:10).

In his first letter to the Corinthian church, Paul wants to make clear to them what the gospel of Jesus Christ really is. In the city of Corinth there were many Greeks. In those days the Greeks were the educated people. It is often the case that intellectually trained people try to explain everything by some sort of systematic rational explanation. Such people have a tendency to fall into a snare, feeling that the only thing that is true or worthy of attention is that which can be logically explained. They say, "What I cannot explain to myself, what I cannot reason out, I just won't believe." And this causes them to have an agnostic attitude. I can understand this, for that is the way I grew up.

> For all the·Athenians and strangers which were there spent their time in nothing else, but either to tell, or to hear some new thing (Acts 17:21).

Where the word *Athenians* is used in the New Testament, one could think of a modern university. Among the people in many universities this intellectual agnosticism is common. Such persons are trapped in the snare of having to explain everything, failing to realize how arrogant that is. When a man says he will have to be able to explain it before he can believe it, he is implying that he knows everything. Such were the people with whom Paul was dealing, and he understood this type of mind very well. He grew up in a Greek city, in Tarsus, and went to school there among such scholars. This very fact caused him to be very simple in his approach.

> And I, brethren, when I came to you, came not with excellency of speech or of wisdom, declaring unto you the testimony of God. For I determined not to know any thing among you, save Jesus Christ, and him crucified (I Cor. 2:1-2).

That word "know" means that Paul was determined that he would not respect anything higher than his simple testimony. He would tell them simply about Jesus Christ, and how His death provided a way out of this world for any believer. This was what Paul was committed to do, and he admits, "And I was with you in weakness, and in fear, and in much trembling" (I Cor. 2:3); because it is a risky thing to talk simple language to sophisticated people.

I can testify from personal experience to such feelings. I have lived on campuses for many many years since I became a Christian. I know very well what the danger is when a believer talks simple language to sophisticated persons. It was my privilege to be a professor in a seminary for twenty-seven years, and I ran into this very experience again and again. I had any number of honest, sincere students sitting in my classrooms that sometimes had to be with me a year or two, or perhaps even three, before they had any confidence in my intellectual ability. Some of them never did discover that because I talked in simple language this did not mean I did not know anything. It was only that I refused to talk in complicated language about the simple things of God, because I had before my mind this very testimony of Paul.

> And I was with you in weakness, and in fear, and in much trembling. And my speech and my preaching was not with enticing words of man's wisdom, but in demonstration of the Spirit and of power: That your faith should not stand in the wisdom of men, but in the power of God (I Cor. 2:3-5).

> There are things true in the gospel that no human mind can grasp.

> Eye hath not seen, nor ear heard, neither have entered into the heart of man, the things which God hath prepared for them that love him (I Cor. 2:9).

The expression "eye hath not seen" covers the whole range of science; just as "nor ear heard" covers the whole range of philosophy; and "neither have entered into the heart of man" refers to all that is meant by art. Nobody in science or philosophy or art has ever seen or heard or imagined the things which God hath prepared for them that love Him. Here is indicated the limitation of reasoning and of logic.

Nothing new was ever discovered by reasoning; all that reason can discover is something you already had in mind. In Paul's day the Greeks were very clever people. Yet no Greek ever guessed that North America was over here, even though the dumbest Indian over here knew it all the time. This demonstrates that what you haven't seen, you cannot find out. What you haven't had some dealings with, you won't ever know. This being the case, how could any man ever know the things of God? No man has ever seen God, no man has ever been with Him. This is why the Holy Spirit is given to us. It is the Spirit that knows all things, even the deep things of God. "But God hath revealed them unto us by his Spirit: for the Spirit searcheth all things, yea, the deep things of God" (I Cor. 2:10). Many of us may not be highly educated, nor know things in any intellectual way, but we can know the gospel. We can know Jesus Christ. And our souls can be saved through Him: even a child can believe and be saved.

17

The Natural Man
Receiveth Not the Things of the Spirit

I Corinthians 2:13-16

Would you have any idea why doubt and unbelief are so common in the world?

But the natural man receiveth not the things of the Spirit of God: for they are foolishness unto him: neither can he know them, because they are spiritually discerned (I Cor. 2:14).

As the apostle Paul continues to discuss the things that have to do with the life of the believer, he is showing the believers in Corinth how very important it is that God gave them the Holy Spirit, to enable them to understand the things of God. This explanation as given by Paul to the Corinthians is still valid today. As we read "the natural man receiveth not the things of the Spirit of God," we are drawn to verse 10, where it is written, "For the Spirit searcheth all things, yea, the deep things of God." In speaking of the things of the Spirit of God, we are thinking of the deep things that He is able to show us.

There are many things that can be known about God that do not require any special help from the Holy Spirit. There is the creation of the world around about us: the stars in the heavens, the mountains, the way the wind blows, and the way the flowers bloom. It can easily be said that God is the Creator and the Keeper of all things without any special spiritual insight. As a matter of fact, no help from the Holy Spirit is needed to think about the reality of God, to realize that God is. As a matter of fact, according to the Bible, it is only a fool who denies it. One does not need the Holy Spirit to know that Christ Jesus died, that He was crucified, was buried, and rose again. That is all a matter of record. Nobody doubts anything about that. No spiritual help is needed to look around in the world and to see that the poor need help, the ignorant need teaching. All that is common knowledge. No doubt God is involved in every one of these facts, but recognizing them does not need any special spiritual insight.

Some will doubt that God is a person. At this point some people get uneasy. There is no doubt the Bible teaches that God is good; in spite of all the sorrow and grief and distress in the world, God is good. And there is no doubt the Bible teaches that God is sovereign; in spite of all the things that happen, the confusion that is all around about us, God is sovereign. There is no doubt that Jesus of Nazareth lived; no one will question that. But that He was born of a virgin, that is another matter! That He was the Son of God, the only begotten Son of God; that there is not another like Him; that He performed supernatural spiritual miracles; the Bible says all this. There need be no question about it! But will men believe it? This is where the questions come in.

That Jesus Christ died on Calvary's cross is a matter of record. But that what He died for was to save sinners, as the substitution for their sins, is what many doubt. Men doubt that Jesus of Nazareth who was laid in the grave actually rose from the dead in bodily form, that He could be handled and seen, that He could take a piece of broiled fish and eat it in front of the people, that He really and truly was alive after three days in the grave. About these affirmations many have unbelief and doubt. Men cannot accept as true that this risen Lord Jesus Christ, forty days later, ascended into heaven, in full view of about one hundred twenty people; that a cloud received Him out of their sight; that there were two men in white there who said to them, "This same Jesus, which is taken up from you into heaven, shall so come in like manner as ye have seen him go into heaven." About this there is unbelief.

People doubt that Christ Jesus is alive now, that He is at the right hand of God, that He is praying for believers at this very moment. If you were to speak of the Holy Spirit, saying that the Holy Spirit came as it is told in Pentecost, that He dwells in believers the way the Bible says He does; if you were to affirm the whole truth of the spiritual world, not only that the Holy Spirit is real, but that angels are, and that heaven is, you would not be believed. If you asserted that Satan is real, that there really is a personal devil, that there really are evil spirits, that there really is a heaven, with a hell as well as a heaven, you would be doubted. If you claimed there will be a resurrection of all men, and then a judgment, people would not believe you, just as they would doubt that there will be eternal blessedness for those that put their trust in the Lord Jesus Christ.

About all these things, Paul would say, "the natural man receiveth not the things of the Spirit of God." These are the deep things of God, of the Spirit of God, "for they are foolishness unto him." In man's way of looking at things, "neither can he know them, because they are spiritually discerned."

It happens that in our family we have been blessed with two living sons. As it happens, each is proficient in science. The older one went into the field of chemistry, earning a Ph.D., and has in recent years given up that profession, finished seminary, and is a pastor in a church in Florida. The other son is in electronics. He is in the general field of electromagnetics and is a consulting engineer. In a recent discussion with an engineering faculty member, he was asked the question: "You don't mean you believe the Bible?" He said, "I do." The other scholar said, "I can't believe it." My son answered: "I can understand that. You could never believe as long as you are the way you are now. To be able to believe you would need to have the grace of God; and anyone can have it." "Whosoever will" could have the grace of God if he wanted it. If a person does not want it, he will not get it. And if he does not get it, he cannot believe. That is all there is to it. How true that is: the natural man cannot believe, but anybody

60

that wants it can be given the grace of God. Without that inward grace to believe, "the natural man receiveth not the things of the Spirit of God; for they are foolishness unto him . . . but they are spiritually discerned." This is precisely one reason why the Holy Spirit is in the world. If anyone is willing, the Holy Spirit will help him to believe what is written about God, even the deep things of God.

18

The Spirit Delivers from Fleshly Sins

I Corinthians 6:9-20

Do you know what argument Paul used to help Christians to turn away from immoral behavior?

What? know ye not that your body is the temple of the Holy Ghost which is in you, which ye have of God, and ye are not your own? For ye are bought with a price: therefore glorify God in your body, and in your spirit, which are God's (I Cor. 6:19-20).

This is Paul's message. Christians consider that carnal sins are wrong, but in that they are not exceptional. Everybody thinks that. When one considers the various types of sinners that are described by Paul: "Neither fornicators, nor idolaters, nor adulterers, nor effeminate, nor abusers of themselves with mankind, Nor thieves, nor covetous, nor drunkards, nor revilers, nor extortioners, shall inherit the kingdom of God (I Cor. 6:9-10), it is obvious nobody is in favor of any of those. Such degenerate conduct is harmful. It will ruin a man's character; it will ruin his personality. Such conduct is harmful physically; it will actually decrease one's energy. The sinner will have a dissipated outlook on life that would be harmful socially: it would break up his family, it would ruin him in the esteem of his friends. Such a way of living would be harmful economically. Such a person would lose his money because he would waste it. That degenerate conduct is always harmful is common knowledge. But knowing this will not cause the sinner to discontinue such behavior.

Often people have felt one of the troubles of mankind is that man is just ignorant. But consider the colleges and universities, look at both faculty and students, are they marked by purity, virtue? As a matter of fact it is notorious that some of the most unusual and the most unhappy developments in our culture have occurred right on the university campus. Willfulness, appetite, and pride are more harmful to any man than his just being ignorant.

Paul introduces an entirely different idea to promote clean conduct among believers. He points out that the body of the believer is the temple of the Holy Spirit. The believer is joined to Christ by the Holy Spirit; and this is a way of saying very soberly, "This is not MY body. It really is OUR body." What is commonly looked upon as my body is the habitation in which I live and in which the Holy Spirit of God lives. Paul writes, "I am crucified with Christ: nevertheless I live; yet not I, but Christ liveth in me" (Gal. 2:20). That is it! This situation is possible by the Holy Spirit. This is what Paul now commends to these Corinthians. "Don't you know that your body is the temple of the Holy Spirit of God?" The believer must not let these be just words; this is real! God really is in the believer, and this is what will make him different. For a believer to think that he is bringing unclean conduct into the very presence of God is a powerful deterrent. He might wish to do this or he might wish to do that, but he will not do it in the presence of God. This is the common experience of true believers.

When it is realized that the Lord Jesus Christ is present Himself in all that I do with myself, I am strengthened by His very presence to obey the Lord. This does not always mean that I wanted to do His will; but it does mean that is what I will do. His presence moves me to act that way. I may still have my old feelings, my old wishes, my old desires, but His presence moves me.

Every now and again we have the testimony of people who have become Christians, who had lived ungodly lives, who were addicted to this or that appetite, so that actually their life was just a miserable experience; they were actually delivered from such bondage by becoming conscious of the fact that the Lord Jesus Himself now was in them. This is a remarkable revelation in Scripture. It will be helpful to realize that if you really want to be helpful to yourself, or really helpful to anybody, young or old, who is having trouble with personal conduct, this passage will guide you:

> Know ye not that the unrighteous shall not inherit the kingdom of God? Be not deceived: neither fornicators, nor idolaters, nor adulterers, nor effeminate, nor abusers of themselves with mankind, Nor thieves, nor covetous, nor drunkards, nor revilers, nor extortioners, shall inherit the kingdom of God. And such were some of you: but ye are washed, but ye are sanctified, but ye are justified in the name of the Lord Jesus, and by the Spirit of our God. All things are lawful unto me, but all things are not expedient: all things are lawful for me, but I will not be brought under the power of any (I Cor. 6:9-12).

Paul does not hold that any particular item of conduct in itself is specially vicious, but anything would be bad if it took control of the believer. The believer is not his own boss. Paul continues:

> Meats for the belly, and the belly for meats: but God shall destroy both it and them. Now the body is not for fornication, but for the Lord; and the Lord for the body. And God hath both raised up the Lord, and will also raise up us by his own power. Know ye not that your bodies are the members of Christ? shall I then take the members of Christ, and make them the members of an harlot? God forbid. What? know ye not that he which is joined to an harlot is one body? for two, saith he, shall be one flesh. But he that is joined unto the Lord is one spirit (I Cor. 6:13-17).

That is the way it reads. This together with the remaining verses is the great argument that Paul uses to help Christians turn away from ungodly, unclean conduct. The believer's body is the very dwelling place of the Holy Spirit of God.

19

The Holy Spirit Enables the Believer to Know Jesus as Lord

I Corinthians 12:1-3

If Jesus of Nazareth is truly the Son of God, why does not everyone know it?

Wherefore I give you to understand, that no man speaking by the Spirit of God calleth Jesus accursed: and that no man can say that Jesus is the Lord, but by the Holy Ghost (I Cor. 12:3).

The gospel presents the simple truth that when a sinner accepts Christ Jesus as Savior and commits himself to Him, he is taken in as a member of the family of God, he is adopted as a child of God. Yet there is much to learn. It is true he belongs, but now he learns. Thus Paul, writing to the Corinthian church, points out that no man speaking by the Spirit of God will ever criticize Jesus Christ. This will never happen. On the other hand, "no man can say that Jesus is the Lord, but by the Holy Ghost." A person cannot really mean such a statement unless the Holy Spirit is helping.

All Christian life and experience depends on Jesus of Nazareth being the Christ. All talk about the word *Christian*, as if that word indicated a certain virtue or a certain character, is misleading. Believers want to be virtuous and they would like to have a strong character, but that is not what makes them believers. The believer is a believer because of Christ Jesus. Christ was the Old Testament title for that Servant of God who would come to save His people; He was to be called "the Christ." When Jesus of Nazareth began His public ministry, He began to teach and to show that He was that Servant. He did the works that Servant was supposed to do, and He worked to set it clearly before the people of His day that He was actually come forth as the Christ, the chosen one of God. He instructed His disciples to go all over the world, and tell all men everywhere that He was the Christ, and to invite them to put their trust in Him that they might be saved.

The message which He gave to His disciples is what we mean by "the gospel." Believers are to take it everywhere, promising salvation to anybody who will believe in Christ Jesus. Christ promised that they would be saved. This gospel is now proclaimed and heard everywhere. I know that many scoff at it, ridicule it, and reject it, but still this is the message: that Jesus of Nazareth is the Christ, the Son of the Living God, and that He can and will save anybody "whosoever will" believe in Him.

There are many people today who want all the blessing of belonging to God: they want the good character and the good name, they want the virtue, they want the kindness, they want the inward peace and joy, they want the consciousness of belonging to God, they want everything; but they don't want the Lord Himself as He is set forth in the Bible. They do not want Jesus of Nazareth. They would like Jesus of Nazareth to be left in a book. They want to read about Him in the Bible, then shut the book. They don't want the presence of the Lord Jesus Christ to be actually with them.

Many people want the blessing of God without the Savior. Paul tells us why this cannot be: "No man can say that Jesus is the Lord, but by the Holy Ghost." If a person does not have the help of the Holy Spirit in his heart, he cannot and will not really believe that

Jesus Christ is Lord of all. Because Christ came into the world to seek and to save the lost, we bring this message to man as a sinner. When the sinner believes this message and accepts Jesus as his Savior, God adopts that sinner as His son. He is now regenerated, born again. Then God sends the Holy Spirit into that believer's heart, enabling him to receive Jesus Christ as his Lord. He is given the inward grace to believe that Jesus of Nazareth is Christ, the Lord, the One chosen to rule. Because of this the believer can now yield, surrender to Him, that He should rule over him. He gives his life over to Christ, accepts the guidance and the direction of the Holy Spirit. This is what Paul meant when he wrote that "no man can say that Jesus is the Lord, but by the Holy Ghost."

The Holy Spirit will enable the believer to yield himself to the will of God, to have the living Lord Jesus Christ within him directing him, moment by moment, day by day. That is not an easy thing to do. For a man or a woman to turn over his or her life to the living Lord Jesus Christ is not easy. The Lord might ask that person to do anything! He might direct that person to go here, there, elsewhere, even when the person may not want to go. Realizing this may happen causes the person to be hesitant. Yet the Holy Spirit can move that person to yield to the point of obeying. The Holy Spirit overcomes the natural reluctance, the natural ideas of self, over-comes these by reminding the believer of Christ Jesus. It is the particular work of the Spirit to take the things of Christ and show them unto the believer. Thus while the Holy Spirit is working in the heart, so that the person is thinking about the Lord Jesus Christ, the Holy Spirit also reminds the believer that Christ Jesus died for sinners. The believer realizes if He had not died for him, he would be lost; and also that now he belongs to Him, he is bought with a price, with the precious blood of the Lamb.

Furthermore the Holy Spirit reminds the believer that the living Lord Jesus Christ is now in the presence of God reconciling him to God. Christ Jesus is now making the believer acceptable to God, so that the believer is there in the presence of God, represented by none other than the beloved Son of God, the Lord Jesus Christ Himself. Also He reminds the believer that the living Lord Jesus

Christ is interceding for him. Every day I can have that in mind. That comes especially close to me if I feel I haven't been doing what I should have been doing. It would be easy for me to feel that living the way I do, and acting the way I do, it could happen that God would simply dismiss me. But He doesn't.

The Holy Spirit reminds me that I have a Savior, who is pleading in glory. Christ is praying for me by the moment. He not only prays for me when I am in difficult situations, He prays for me before I get into them, just as He prays for me after I have been in them. He is constantly interceding on my behalf. To realize this affects me. The Holy Spirit also shows me how Christ Jesus loves me, that He actually cares for me and actually puts Himself out for me. It is no wonder then that I love Him because He first loved me. And because Christ Jesus gave Himself for me, I find it in me to give myself to Him. That is why, if I have the Holy Spirit in me, I can say that for me Christ Jesus is Lord, and I will gladly acknowledge Him as my Lord and Master.

20

The Spirit Enables a Believer to Serve

I Corinthians 12:4-7

Do you realize that there are special spiritual gifts which enable a believer to serve as a member of the body of Christ?

Now there are diversities of gifts, but the same Spirit. And there are differences of administrations, but the same Lord.

And there are diversities of operations, but it is the same God which worketh all in all. But the manifestation of the Spirit is given to every man to profit withal (I Cor. 12:4-7).

Thus Paul sketches the various activities that are carried on by individual members of the body of Christ. Each member of the body of Christ may have some gift, and each one will be directed by the Spirit of God. Each one may perform a function in the body of Christ. Though there are many gifts and many different ways of doing things, all differ, and yet they all cooperate for a common good. As an illustration, look at your hand. Do you notice how different the fingers are? They are set in different locations and in different positions. They are different lengths and thicknesses. They have differing strength, and yet they work together, because they are in one hand. The hand as a whole can do many things that any one finger alone cannot do.

There is a very real sense in which the fellowship of believers accomplishes some things in the will of God and in the work of Jesus Christ beyond what any individual believer alone could do. There are special meanings in this term *the body of Christ.* Scripture indicates there are diversities of gifts and of administrations and operations; yet there is evidence of the Spirit given one way to one member and another way to another member, even though the Spirit is for everybody.

Service in the body of Christ is not by natural gifts. There are natural gifts, such as when some man has a strong physique. Sometimes there is a man that is tall, broad shouldered, athletically inclined, physically fit: that would be a tremendous benefit. He would have great advantage. Then there are persons with administrative ability who have a knack for getting things done. Some people possess means. They did nothing to earn such, but they have it. They received their money just as they received the color of their eyes; they were born with it. It is now their fortune which they can use. Such natural gifts can be used in serving the Lord. Yet this is not what Paul is talking about when he discusses such enablements in I Corinthians, chapters 12-14. Sometimes students label such a gift as Paul mentions as "charisma." This is a Greek word that actually means "spiritual," but it does not say what it is. Such gifts can be thought of as "divine enablements for service": divine (coming from God) enablements (they enable the person to serve) which can be employed with skill and with strength to advantage. They are given severally, not all to the same person, but to different believers, some here, some there. But they are always given for one common purpose, that of fitting the body for serving the Lord.

When considering the gifts of the Spirit throughout the whole church, we can learn a great deal by just reading what Paul has to say about them. When people use the term *gifts of the Spirit* they are generally referring to what Paul is discussing in the Corinthian epistle. In writing in I Corinthians 12:4-6 Paul makes three similar comments: in verse 4, "There are diversities of gifts, but the same Spirit"; in verse 5, "There are differences of administration, but the same Lord"; and in verse 6, "There are diversities of operations, but it is the same God which worketh all in all." In these three verses in succession, we find "Spirit" in verse 4, "Lord" in verse 5, "God" in verse 6. Thus the Trinity is in verses 4, 5, and 6. Let us note that these gifts are spoken of as enablements. They are given to the believer to make it possible for him to do something. They are capacities that are given to the believer, who does not earn them. He does not develop them. They are given to each individual at the will of God.

In the seventh verse it is written that "the manifestation of the Spirit is given to every man to profit withal." This means that everybody is to profit. These gifts are received after one becomes a believer. This means that a person who becomes a believer and enters into the fellowship of Christian people may receive one of these gifts or more, with which to serve the group as a whole. Each member is responsible to everyone else for the proper use of his gift. By this method the Holy Spirit enables the believer to serve in the body of Christ.

21

The Spirit Divides the Gifts Among Believers

I Corinthians 12:8-14

Do you understand how a Christian could do things in the power of the Spirit that he would never be able to do in his own strength? Christians are often different in their conduct from what one would ordinarily expect, because they are helped to go beyond their own capacity or their own human nature. Paul talks about this when he writes:

> For to one [that is to a believer] is given by the Spirit the word of wisdom; to another the word of knowledge by the same Spirit; To another faith by the same Spirit; to another the gifts of healing by the same Spirit; To another the working of miracles; to another prophecy; to another discerning of spirits; to another divers kinds of tongues; to another the interpretation of tongues: But all these worketh that one and the selfsame Spirit, dividing to every man severally as he will (I Cor. 12:8-11).

Thus believers are given capacities greater than their own from the Spirit of God to serve Him. It is important to note that these gifts are for the purpose of serving, of helping others. These capacities are called "gifts," because they are given to the believers. Believers do not earn them, nor qualify for them, nor work for them. They are received as gifts. A good description of the word *gift* is that it is a divine enablement for service; God giving the believer a certain capacity to accomplish things for Him.

The first gift mentioned is "the word of wisdom." Some believers have an understanding of just how the truth that they have learned should apply. They have a way of understanding what happens round about them, just as if all was written out before them. They have the understanding and the thoughts of wisdom. Another gift mentioned is "the word of knowledge." Knowledge and wisdom are not quite the same. Knowledge is the ability to call to mind all the various things which are known. There are those who cannot remember anything that might be pertinent to any issue at hand. The Holy Spirit gives to some believers the word of knowledge. Wisdom can be called human good sense. Knowledge can be thought to be among other things a good mind.

The third gift mentioned is more readily recognized: that is the one called faith. This is not the kind of faith involved when a person becomes a believer. It is the kind of faith whereby a believer sees results because of his belief in God. God has given His promises to believers. As the believer understands and believes the promises of God he expects things to come to pass because God said they would. The believer believes in Him and trusts in Him and results come to pass. Such are acts of faith, works of faith. There are persons that have this gift in prayer and meditation when they yield themselves to be led by the Spirit.

The next gift mentioned is "the gifts of healing by the same Spirit." It should be noted "the gifts of healing" is the expression by which this capacity is referred to each time. This is not healing; it is the gifts of healing. That is to say, here is a man, John Smith, who is a believer. Here is another man, Tom Brown, who is sick, or is in some way physically handicapped: physically hurting or in physical illness of some sort. John Smith has in himself a certain gift given to him of God by which he can exercise his faith concerning Tom Brown's body, so that consequences of healing appear. There is much talk about healing by faith one way or another, but Scripture recognizes the fact as real. There are persons who in response to the Word of God and in keeping with the promises of God and guided by the Holy Spirit actually are given the capacity of praying for the healing of the body of someone else, so that results follow. There are too many of these instances to ignore them. There can be no doubt that such things as the gifts of healing actually exist. Not every believer has them, but any one believer may have them at any one time as God will give them to him.

The next gift mentioned is "to another the working of miracles." This could well require a whole study of its own. Recently I prepared a booklet entitled "I Believe in Miracles," in which I discuss this gift in greater detail. There are persons who have the capacity given to them that enables them to ask God for some certain thing to happen, which will then happen because God brings it to pass.

It is similar to the next gift, which is called "prophecy," or "interpreting of Scripture." Not everyone can interpret Scripture. Reading it and studying it does not guarantee that one will understand it. To interpret Scripture requires that one understands the meaning that the Holy Spirit had in mind. To recall verses from Scripture, and to have these verses in mind in such a way that the meaning and truth in them becomes clear is a capacity that God gives to some believers in a special way.

The next gift in this list, "the discerning of spirits," is one we know very little about. Some believers seem to have a capacity of being able to discern the spirit in another man. They seem to know whether that spirit really seeks to serve and honor the Lord Jesus Christ, or whether that spirit is a selfish spirit that is actually sinful.

Then again Paul refers to a gift many do not understand: "to another divers kinds of tongues." This is a manifestation that is generally obscure. It is so often not clear to sincere observers whether what they see and hear is actually "speaking in tongues." I personally see no reason why I should not believe it. Many people will say that the speaking in tongues noted in the Book of Acts is different. I am personally inclined to think so. When the disciples were speaking in tongues at Pentecost everyone understood them. But in the speaking in tongues which occurs in churches today in various parts of the country, no one seems to understand what is being said. From what Paul writes to the Corinthians, it is apparent that they did not understand what was being uttered. I get the impression that what is going on in the churches today is very much like what was happening among the Corinthians, rather than what happened at Pentecost.

There are still other people who have the capacity for "the interpretation of tongues." All these are divine enablements given to the individual believers, not to everybody but to some, for service. Not one of these gifts is a personal attribute. No believer is that smart, or that good; but "all these worketh that one and selfsame Spirit, dividing to every man severally as he will" (I Cor. 12:11).

Not one of these gifts was ever to be exercised for the believer's own personal interest. Each one was to be used in service to help others. This means that no believer becomes stronger or smarter because he has any of these gifts; but through his yielded heart the Lord is able to operate in power through that person to bless others. Such gifts may seem to be unreal to those who do not have them, but they can be genuine and they can be valid and living. It is true the claim that a believer has such gifts may cause much misgivings and doubt, but other believers would be wise to remember that such gifts can be actually genuine. A person can be a believer without having any gift, but if he has such an enablement, he is to exercise it for the sake of other people.

22

Believers Should Not Compare
Themselves by Gifts

I Corinthians 12:15-30

Do you realize that it is quite unwise to rate one believer above another because of the work that he performs in the church? We are considering just now various aspects of the truth of the Holy Spirit of God, and we are trying to understand how the Holy Spirit is involved in the life and experience of a believer. In I Corinthians 12:15-30 Paul points out that no matter what gifts he may have, no believer should think he is better than any other believer. He should not think that he is smarter than any other believer because the Lord happens to use him to accomplish certain purposes.

Paul presents a simple yet quite clear argument to show why no believer should ever feel superior to other believers. He uses the figure of the body as the believer's way of obeying the Lord. Throughout this discussion he makes it clear that the Lord is the head, and believers are members of the body. Paul had pointed out that the Holy Spirit of God gives to individual believers certain capacities, called gifts. These gifts vary from each other, but actually they belong to each other. He writes, "If the foot shall say, Because I am not the hand, I am not of the body; is it therefore not of the body? And if the ear shall say, Because I am not the eye, I am not of the body; is it therefore not of the body?" (I Cor. 12:15-16). There is a real difference in the ear and the eye. They function as two entirely different operations. But Paul is asking, does this make any difference? Do you think that anyone saying he does not belong is actually going to change the situation at all?

Paul asks, "If the whole body were an eye, where were the hearing?" (I Cor. 12:17). That is a way of saying that so far as the body is concerned, it needs the eye, but it also needs the hearing. "If the whole were hearing, where were the smelling?" The body needs these various organs so that it may function effectively. "But now hath God set the members every one of them in the body, as it hath pleased him" (I Cor. 12:18). So you have two ears, and you have two eyes, and you have a nose, and you have a mouth, each one with its own function. Likewise there are all different kinds of believers, each one of them having his own function.

> And if they were all one member, where were the body? And now are they many members, yet but one body. And the eye cannot say unto the hand, I have no need of thee: nor again the head to the feet, I have no need of you (I Cor. 12:19-21).

In other words, there is a difference in these gifts, yes; but they are not separate. Just because they are different does not separate them from each other. Each serves a needed function. The eye sees, the ear hears, the nose smells, the hands hold, the shoulder carries, as the case may be, and so on.

> Nay, much more those members of the body, which seem to be more feeble, are necessary: And those members of the body, which we think to be less honourable, upon these we bestow more abundant honour; and our uncomely parts have more abundant comeliness (I Cor. 12:22-23).

I think the apostle is pointing out that every part of the body counts. Whoever is sharing this, whether you are Episcopalian, Presbyterian, Methodist, Baptist, Pentecostal, Salvation Army, you all belong. It would be a mighty poor day in the church when a Presbyterian would say that because that man is a Baptist he is not a full-fledged believer; or a Methodist would say that because that person over there belongs to the Salvation Army he is not a believer. The Lord would never do that.

Paul argues that a hand and a foot and an eye and an ear and a nose are different aspects of one body. Because they are different from each other does not mean that they are separate from each other.

That there should be no schism in the body; but that the members should have the same care one for another (I Cor. 12:25).

The Lord does not look with favor upon any believer separating himself from other believers. It does not mean all must be alike. One believer may be an ear who listens or another may be a mouth who talks. All do not have to be the same. But because one does a different thing does not mean he is different from the others. Believers should care for each other.

And whether one member suffer, all the members suffer with it; or one member be honoured, all the members rejoice with it (I Cor. 12:26).

Every believer should take this very seriously to heart. Each believer living obediently in the Spirit should pray for those believers who are in some division and who are hurting. Believers should be very careful not to gloat over the misfortunes of other groups of believers. That would not be pleasing to the Lord. Believers all belong to the Lord in His name. They should not let their differences separate them from each other, for they are all members of one body. The Holy Spirit makes believers to differ from each other, not so that each will be separate, and not so that one believer is better than another, but that all believers might serve each other. "Now ye are the body of Christ, and members in particular."

And God hath set some in the church, first apostles, secondarily prophets, thirdly teachers, after that miracles, then gifts of healings, helps, governments, diversities of tongues (I Cor. 12:28).

Paul raises the question: "Are all apostles?" Of course not! "Are all prophets?" No! "Are all teachers? Are all workers of miracles?" Why, no! "Have all the gifts of healing?" That is not to be expected. "Do all speak with tongues?" No! "Do all interpret?" No! "But covet earnestly the best gifts." The fact is, gifts differ. If there are some that are "best," there must be some that are "better" and some that are "good." "And yet show I unto you a more excellent way." Then Paul goes on in chapter 13 to show believers a more excellent way of achieving the service of the Lord than by gifts. It is proper to seek earnestly the "best" gift, though a man may receive a lesser gift. He should seek the better, and never boast of any. The gifts are never for pride, nor pleasure, but they are for the profit of others.

23

Gifts Are Given for the Purpose of Helping Others

I Corinthians 14

Do you know that though Christians receive gifts for service in a special way from the living Lord Jesus Christ, the use of these gifts should be directed by good common sense? It is such a common thing to feel that when a person has been endowed with any gift of the Spirit, he is in a class by himself. This of course is not true. That person is not any different in himself and is just as responsible to use good common sense as anyone else. He should use the gifts of the Spirit whether they are gifts in praying or in interpreting Scripture. Such gifts are no different than gifts of physical strength or intellectual brilliance. They should be kept under control and used for God's glory. Good judgment should guide the believer.

Gifts will vary in importance: some are better, some of them are best. The importance varies according to how useful these gifts are in helping others. Spiritual gifts are not for the believer's personal enjoyment. They are not his in order to make him proud, nor because he especially deserves them. They are capacities that are given to him that he might be able to help others.

Paul emphasizes this truth in his argument in the fourteenth chapter of I Corinthians. When he points out that gifts vary in importance because of how they will help others, he draws attention to the difference between "speaking in tongues" and "prophesying." The word "prophesy" does not mean especially to predict; rather it means to interpret Scripture. Paul writes:

> For he that speaketh in an unknown tongue speaketh not unto men, but unto God: for no man understandeth him; howbeit in the spirit he speaketh mysteries (I Cor. 14:2).

The chances are that what the believer may be saying may be known to God. "But he that prophesieth speaketh unto men," not men of the world, not just any natural man, but other believers, people who are believers; and he speaketh unto the other men in the body of Christ "to edification, and exhortation, and comfort" (I Cor. 14:3). Then he goes on to say, "He that speaketh in an unknown tongue edifieth himself; but he that prophesieth edifieth the church." Verse 3 in a remarkable way indicates the three functions that a person teaching will actually perform: to *edify* is to build up faith, to *exhort* is to encourage service, and to *comfort* is to strengthen the believer. The person who is interpreting Scripture will do those things. He will edify people if he interprets Scripture truly, he will strengthen their faith, he will exhort them to serve the Lord, and he will comfort them in the will of God.

In verse 4 Paul points out: "He that speaketh in an unknown tongue edifieth himself." The believer himself is the only one getting any benefit, "but he that prophesieth edifieth the church." The discussion continues from verses 5 to 12. It is really a classic argument. Paul could have said, "This is right; that is wrong." But he wants the believers in Corinth to think and to reason. He wants them to exercise good common sense. They will need that in trying to live the life of faith. In the course of his discussion Paul writes, "I would that ye all spake with tongues"; by this he meant to say, "I would be very glad to have every one of you affected by the Holy Spirit in such a way that you could speak in tongues." He continues, "But rather that ye prophesied," meaning "I would rather have you able to interpret Scripture." Then again Paul writes, "For greater is he that prophesieth than he that speaketh with tongues," meaning to say, "he is of greater significance, greater value." ". . . except he interpret, that the church may receive edifying." Gifts are to be used to help others.

"Now, brethren, if I come unto you speaking with tongues, what shall I profit you, except I shall speak to you either by revelation, or by knowledge, or by prophesying, or by doctrine?" (I Cor. 13:6). If I fail to speak in such a way that you can understand me, what good will it do? "And even things without life giving sound, whether pipe or harp [substitute organ or piano], except they give a distinction in the sounds [if you failed to hear the various notes], how shall it be known what is piped or harped? For if the trumpet give an uncertain sound, who shall prepare himself to the battle? So likewise ye, except ye utter by the tongue words easy to be understood, how shall it be known what is spoken? for ye shall speak into the air" (I Cor. 14:7-9).

I was for many years a professor of Bible in a seminary, trying to help young men prepare themselves for the ministry. We had the students preach before us, and then we criticized them. No doubt we criticized them in various ways, but there was one thing we often used to point out: "except ye utter by the tongue words easy to be understood, how shall it be known what is spoken? Ye shall speak into the air." I am afraid there was many a preacher who got out of seminary who never learned that lesson.

It may be there are so many kinds of voices in the world and none of them is without significance. Paul continues his discussion, "Therefore if I know not the meaning of the voice [if I hear a man talking but do not know what he is saying], I shall be unto him that speaketh a barbarian." He is speaking and I do no understand. He looks on me as if I were a foreigner, a barbarian. "And he that speaketh shall be a barbarian unto me." I am sure some of you know what it is when you listen to a man speaking, and another asks you, "Do you understand him?" And you will have to admit, "No!

Everything he says is Greek to me." Well, that is exactly the idea here.

"Even so ye, forasmuch as ye are zealous of spiritual gifts, seek that ye may excel to the edifying of the church" (I Cor. 14:12). "Seek that ye may excel" in your exercise of the gifts, "to the edifying of the church." Paul goes on to say, "Wherefore let him that speaketh in an unknown tongue pray that he may interpret" (I Cor. 14:13). If it should be that a believer has this gift, that he does speak with tongues, he should make it a matter of prayer, that God will give him the gift to interpret; to explain to people what it is that is happening. "For if I pray in an unknown tongue, my spirit prayeth [there need be no doubt about that], but my understanding is unfruitful. What is it then? I will pray with the spirit, and I will pray with the understanding also" (I Cor. 14:14-15a). It is in prayer, as it is in preaching. A person should pray in a way that the people hearing him can follow and understand him. "I will sing with the spirit, and I will sing with the understanding also. Else when thou shalt bless with the spirit [that is praying with the spirit], how shall he that occupieth the room of the unlearned say Amen at thy giving of thanks, seeing he understandeth not what thou sayest? For thou verily givest thanks well, but the other is not edified" (I Cor. 14:15b-17). Paul is willing to concede that praying may be genuine and good, and yet the other may not be edified; this praying may not help the other man. "I thank my God, I speak with tongues more than ye all." This statement has caused problems of interpretation. Why not just take it as it reads? Paul was greatly blessed in such manifestations of the Spirit in his own experience, but he points out: "Yet in the church I had rather speak five words with my understanding, that by my voice I might teach others also, than ten thousand words in an unknown tongue" (I Cor. 14:19). Paul would have preferred his praying to be in five words with his understanding that he might help others. This demonstrates the whole point in his discussion.

24

The Spirit Writes the Word of Christ upon the Heart of the Believer

II Corinthians 3:3

Can you see how a believer can be an epistle of Christ? It is always helpful to face the issue: "What is the gospel, according to you?" Many have heard that question, and have felt uncomfortable at times. But this is a proper question that anyone could ask a believer.

In continuing to search for what the apostle Paul says about the Holy Spirit and His relation to the believer, we look just now at his words:

Forasmuch as ye are manifestly declared to be the epistle of Christ ministered by us, written not with ink, but with the Spirit of the living God; not in tables of stone, but in fleshy tables of the heart (II Cor. 3:3).

Believers were to be thought of as epistles of Christ, written by the Holy Spirit on the hearts of the believers. This is how believers show the gospel to the world. The world outside will never know the good news if believers do not tell it. It is for believers to go and tell them; to be witnesses unto Christ.

Christ Jesus, the Son of God, came into this world to offer Himself a ransom for many. He offered Himself in the place of the sinner, as a substitute. God has arranged it that "whosoever will may come, and whosoever believeth in Him shall not perish but have everlasting life."

Faith in Christ Jesus is the key to spiritual blessing. Faith in Him is the way in which believers are identified with Christ. The believer commits himself to Him, actually joins with Christ in His death, His burial, and in His resurrection, as well as His communion with God, and thus shares as a joint-heir with Christ Jesus.

When Christ Jesus came into the world, He did not demonstrate something that any human being could imitate so that he might be like Christ. Rather, He did something that I am to share. If I am to share the life of Christ through faith, I must believe in Him. When I believe in Him, I belong to God. I am made a child of God, I am born again by the grace and the power of God, and He gives His Holy Spirit to live in me. Paul is saying in II Corinthians 3:3 that if I thus belong to the Lord then I am "a letter, an epistle of Christ" for the public to read. If this is so, as I share the life of Christ it should show. Something should happen in me for the world to see that I belong in Christ Jesus. If the gospel were only in words, then tablets of stone would have sufficed. A person could have memorized it and shared it. But that would not be the gospel.

The truth of the Lord Jesus Christ is never fully set forth in so many words; the truth in the Lord Jesus Christ is to be seen in a new relationship. I accept the Lord and commit myself to Him, I am adopted as a child of the family of God, and the living God begins to have dealings with me. All this results in a new relationship and this should be manifested in new action. It is not something that is read; it is something that is seen. The inner response in the heart of the believer to the will of God and to the Word of God is by the operation of the Holy Spirit in the believer. Paul points out this will show up in the believer, so that people can see it. When a person believes in the Lord Jesus Christ, the Holy Spirit takes the things of Christ and activates them in that person so they will show in his conduct. The believer shows the truth that he belongs to God and that God is in him. His conduct reveals a personal communion and fellowship with Christ.

In the case of a believer it is not a matter of what he says about God. We only need to watch the believer: how does he pray? If a believer does not pray, then all the talking he may do will not mean much. How does he use the Sabbath Day? If he fails to worship God, no amount of talk on his part will help. No one will pay any attention to him. It is the outward action that shows the inward reality so far as a believer is concerned. Does the believer reverence God? Is He first in that person's life? How could people ever know that? People can see how he orders his time. What does he do on Sunday? Does he ever read the Bible? Does he ever pray? How does the believer act toward authority? Does he obey the laws of the land? How does he treat his neighbors? Is he considerate of them? Such a person can talk about the rights of people and the freedom of this country, but if he is a selfish man in his conduct, everything he says falls flat. As a believer, how does he act toward the poor? Does he give to the poor? If it is characteristic of that person to give to the poor, in so doing he acts like the Lord Jesus Christ, who came to give Himself for us. The same is true of the church. How much does that person give to the program? How much does that person share in the worship of the church? In a believer's conduct action speaks louder than words. The believer is an epistle, known and read of men. The Holy Spirit will write the will of the Lord Jesus Christ on his heart.

25

The Holy Spirit Changes the Believer into the Image of Christ

II Corinthians 3:17-18

Have you ever noticed how a real believer wants no credit for any godliness in his conduct? Do you feel that you know what causes a man who believes in Christ to grow in grace and in knowledge? Many different times I have had people ask me, "How can I grow as a Christian? What can I do so that as the days go by I will become more acceptable and more useful to the Lord?" The apostle Paul speaks to this point when he points out how the Holy Spirit will affect the developing of the Christian life.

Now the Lord is that Spirit: and where the Spirit of the Lord is, there is liberty. But we all, with open face beholding as in a glass the glory of the Lord, are changed into the same image from glory to glory, even as by the Spirit of the Lord (II Cor. 3:17-18).

Believers looking up into the presence of the Lord, looking into the glory of the Lord Jesus Christ, "are changed into the same image from glory to glory, even as by the Spirit of the Lord." Here is the secret. To share in this wonderful truth, one would have to believe in the Lord Jesus Christ and have committed himself to Him. Changes will take place when a person receives the truth of the Lord Jesus Christ into his heart and takes it to be real. There is nothing hidden about becoming a believer. It makes as much sense as getting off a sinking boat and into the lifeboat.

How would a person grow as a believer? By gazing upon the face of the Lord Jesus Christ. The more a believer looks at Him, the more he will love Him. "He is the fairest of ten thousand to my soul." If a believer comes to the Lord Jesus Christ and really turns to Him, the first glimpse he will have of Him is on Calvary's cross. The great truth of Calvary's cross is that He died for each person. Pausing here will do profound things for the believer. A believer will realize that he has been bought with a price. The great Son of God gave Himself for each person.

After the believer has thoroughly grasped that, then comes the wonderful truth that if a person really and truly believes, he knows he is not his own. He knows he has been bought and paid for. The believer realizes that it is in God's plan that he should be dead to the things of this world in Christ Jesus. He should yield, let go of everything, just as if he were dead. A dead man cannot take anything with him. One does not take anything of this world into the believer's experience. The believer reckons himself to be dead. He has to let go of things and turn himself over to God. Then the believer will be brought into the very presence of God. He will be raised from the dead by the Holy Spirit of God and God will pour His Holy Spirit into his heart. The believer will actually have the Lord Jesus Christ within himself and that will certainly make a difference.

Someone may say, "I don't see how it will make any difference if I have the Lord Jesus Christ." This is like saying you wouldn't see it make any difference if you brought a light into a dark room. You know there would be a difference. That is the way it will be in a believer's heart. Oh, the chairs, the table, and the stove will be there just as they always were. But the believer will have a whole new frame of mind. Things just look different when the light is turned on. So it is with our spiritual experience as one comes "out of darkness into His marvelous light."

Belonging to the Lord Jesus Christ and having this fellowship with Him is not self-induced. The believer does not get to be like the Lord Jesus Christ by imitating Him: walking, talking, acting as He did. Consider He died for you, so it is as if He reached out His hand to you. What happens next? The believer takes hold of His hand. He looks up and takes hold of Christ. He commits himself to Him, and when he does, Christ lifts him out of himself. Christ will give him His Word of promise. God will forgive him for Christ's sake. This is what He has arranged for believers, and all of this happened at the cross of Calvary. We sing, "At the cross, at the cross, where I first saw the light; and the burden of my heart rolled away"; and that is exactly what happened when I yielded. I reckoned myself dead.

When Christ raises the believer from the dead, that person will be different. He will be a new man in Christ Jesus. Christ Jesus will give him the Holy Spirit. This Holy Spirit is actually a person who will show the believer the things of Christ. The believer is after that never alone, never again shut away from the personal presence of the living Lord Jesus Christ. The believer is "changed into the same image from glory to glory, even as by the Spirit of the Lord."

This is personally experienced, in much the same way as the

Lord's Supper is shared. One of the significant things about the Lord's Supper is that each individual believer eats the bread. *I* open *my* mouth and put the bread in *my* mouth and *I* eat the bread. This is a marvelous symbol of the fact *I* received Jesus Christ as *my* personal Savior. In the same way *I* drink the cup: *I* pick it up out of its tray, and *I* hold it in *my* hands and *I* put it to *my* mouth and *I* drink it. This is the way the believer receives the Holy Spirit of God. All the believer does is open his heart and the Holy Spirit will come in and be there with him. The believer is prompted to gaze on the Lord, to look at Him, to look into His presence, and to seek the Lord Jesus Christ. The person himself does not do this. It is "Christ in you, the hope of glory." The believer may not even know it is happening. The neighbors will know. His family will know. It is like a flower opening up, under His grace, when the Holy Spirit shows the believer the things of Christ.

26

Receiving the Holy Spirit Is the Beginning of the Life of Faith

Galatians 3:1-5

Becoming a believer in Christ means more than just making a decision. It involves something like getting married. When a man and a woman come together with the prospects of getting married they usually follow certain stages: first, they get acquainted with each other—this may take a shorter or longer time. Then there is a period that was once called courtship; now it is said that they are running around together or going steady. Then comes a moment when there is commitment to each other in what is called in a formal way, betrothal or engagement. This is a definite stage of the fellowship; finally comes the wedding day. This is the way it happens when two are getting married, and it is not much different in becoming a Christian.

First, a person learns about the gospel and after it is understood and believed, then there is a personal commitment to the Lord which is like a wedding. There is normally a development in the mind in becoming a believer, as well as a certain changing of attitude. Usually a person begins to think about God and Christ and such reflections are stages one passes through; but all of this is only incidental to the real thing. It is associated with accepting Christ, involved in it; but it is not really what happens when one becomes a believer. Just as no one can become married by himself, so no one can become a believer in himself, by simply adopting certain views or accepting certain ideas. I did not become a believer because I finally agreed with all believers; I did not become a believer because I started acting like a believer.

When I became a believer something happened between me and Jesus Christ, and He came to be with me. What really happened was that I heard the gospel story and I accepted Him as my Savior by putting my trust in Him and counting on Him to do as He promised. Then God accepted me and I was adopted as a child of God. Because I have been adopted as a child of God, He has done something for me: God has sent His Holy Spirit into my heart so that I actually now am a person who has dwelling in him—living in him—the Holy Spirit of God. And living as a believer on my part is my response to this indwelling Christ.

Paul discusses all this in the Book of Galatians. In Galatians 3:1-5 there is a reference to the fact that receiving the Holy Spirit into the heart is the beginning of the life of faith. Paul reminds these believers:

O foolish Galatians, who hath bewitched you, that ye should not obey the truth, before whose eyes Jesus Christ hath been evidently set forth, crucified among you? (Gal. 3:1).

In these words Paul points out how the gospel was preached in presenting the truth about "Christ Jesus crucified" among them. You will note Paul did not begin by bringing in something that they were to do. Nor is the gospel preached by having a discussion of some changes that should take place in the community. The gospel is preached when the truth of the Lord Jesus Christ, as set forth in His earthly life and recorded in the Bible, is actually presented to the heart; how Christ Jesus the Son of God died for sinners and was buried and rose again.

All that is reported about Jesus Christ in the gospel had been "evidently set forth": "evidently" meaning "by evidence." Certain things had been done in demonstration of the reality of what was being preached, and were offered as evidence to support the preaching of the gospel. This truth that the Lord Jesus Christ had been crucified for them was preached among them in such a way that demonstrations to commend its reality were actually presented along with the preaching.

What might such a demonstration be? To begin with, there could have been various aspects of self-denial. Together with the preaching of the gospel there could have been instances of self-denial set forth, which these Galatians had seen happen. They may have noted some believers as witnesses and as preachers and may have observed their conduct as clear evidence that they were people who were testifying to their faith in the Lord. Such testimony had been set before them by way of evidence so that they could understand that the first thing a believer does is yield to the Lord Jesus Christ, denying self, so that he is raised from the dead by the grace of God. This sort of conduct might have been demonstrated in a practical fashion before them from time to time.

> This only would I learn of you, Received ye the Spirit by the works of the law, or by the hearing of faith? (Gal. 3:2)

Apparently receiving the Spirit occurred as the culmination of the gospel preaching. When any witness was preaching the gospel and telling about the Lord Jesus Christ, he would begin by telling about Christ Jesus being crucified. He would declare that Christ was laid in the grave as He carried away the sins of the whole world. But he would not stop with that; he would go on to tell how He was raised from the dead, and after showing Himself alive by many infallible proofs, He ascended into heaven, where He is now at the right hand of God. From thence He poured forth the Holy Spirit. As all this truth was presented it would be obvious that the pouring forth of the Holy Spirit was the culmination of the person's becoming a believer.

It seems clear that when a person becomes a believer he first hears that Christ Jesus died for him. As a natural man in the presence of God the soul is before Him as a sinner. The gospel is brought to this sinner when he is told that Christ Jesus died for his sins. Spiritual life for the natural man begins by his accepting Christ Jesus as his Savior from his sins. He can rejoice to know that when he confesses his sins they are carried away in Christ Jesus. Then he also learns that Christ Jesus was raised from the dead and because Christ was raised from the dead the believer will live also. Then he will be helped to understand that God will receive him in Christ Jesus and count him as though he had died and had been raised from the dead.

Becoming a believer is not a matter of starting out to do the right thing, nor is it a life merely of submission: as one could start by yielding to God in certain circumstances so that one is a nice person who is humble and ready to fit into things. A person becomes a believer by receiving Christ Jesus and yielding himself to Him, receiving the Holy Spirit of God and being led in obedience to God. We have noted in Galatians 3:2 that believers had received the Spirit not by the works of the law. A person does not qualify for receiving the Spirit by pious conduct; he accepts Him by faith. It is also not merely by adopting an attitude but by hearing the Word of God that the soul can understand it and believe what God has promised; and in this way the Holy Spirit is received.

Are ye so foolish? having begun in the Spirit, are ye now made perfect by the flesh? (Gal. 3:3)

Paul reminds them they began in the Spirit. First of all the Holy Spirit showed them how Christ Jesus called them: so they came. The

Holy Spirit showed them that Christ Jesus died for their sins: so they confessed their sins. The Holy Spirit showed them that in their own hearts they were inclined to be sinful: so they repented. The Holy Spirit showed them that Christ Jesus died for them: so they accepted.

This whole process begins in the Spirit. Paul challenges them to see that they would not now be made "perfect," that is, "mature," by any procedures of the flesh. Would they become mature by controlling their conduct, managing themselves, doing the right things? or would they not become perfect, or mature, by the hearing of the Spirit? Since they began in the Spirit, they would continue in the Spirit. In other words, the believer grows into consistent conduct, not by rules but by believing in the Lord Jesus Christ.

Paul carries on the argument:

> Have ye suffered so many things in vain? if it be yet in vain (Gal. 3:4).

The suffering had been in self-denial and in self-crucifixion. They had become believers and they had received the Holy Spirit that way; were all those things for nothing? Would they now have to live according to certain rules and regulations?

> He therefore that ministereth to you the Spirit, and worketh miracles among you, doeth he it by the works of the law, or by the hearing of faith? (Gal. 3:5)

A minister is supposed to minister the Holy Spirit to the believers; in his preaching and teaching he is supposed to share the Holy Spirit with his people, not by telling them what to do—which would be according to the law—but by telling people what God will do according to His grace.

27

The Promise of the Holy Spirit
in the Blessing of Abraham

Galatians 3:13-14

Do you realize that above all else Abraham was promised the presence of God?

> Christ hath redeemed us from the curse of the law, being made a curse for us: for it is written, Cursed is every one that hangeth on a tree: That the blessing of Abraham might come on the Gentiles through Jesus Christ; that we might receive the promise of the Spirit through faith (Gal. 3:13-14).

Notice how these words go together, especially in the two clauses in that last verse. Actually the "blessing of Abraham" and the "promise of the Spirit through faith" are statements of the same thing.

It was written in the covenant of Abraham, "I will bless thee and make thee a blessing." Abraham was counted as "the friend of God." Many have understood that because of that covenant he would be given the land of Canaan; and this was true. But being given the land of Canaan just showed the real truth, for as Abraham was given the land of Canaan, the believer in God will be given the promises of God and His blessing. God would personally prepare benefits in grace that would be given to those who put their trust in Him and all these benefits would involve His own presence.

The blessing of Abraham is not to be seen so much in the land, as in the promise: "I will bless thee and make thee a blessing": the Lord Himself would be there with Abraham. In the New Testament we have received the promise of the Spirit through faith, and now the Spirit takes the things of Christ and shows them unto us. What the Holy Spirit does in the heart of a believer is to make him conscious of the presence of God. And this is what was promised in the beginning. The covenant with Abraham indicated that God would personally prepare and provide benefits in grace, all of which would be involved in His own personal presence. He offers to come and to bless the man who puts his trust in Him.

The covenant of Abraham featured this great truth: in blessings and in the benefits that come in life as one believes in God, the primary mover is God, not man. Blessing and benefits will come because of what God will give, not because of what man will earn. The believer's part is to receive what God has done for him, is doing with him, and will do to him. "I will bless him that blesses you and curse him that curses you" is the way the Old Testament reports the covenant of Abraham. God will thus personally identify Himself with His people who believe in Him. Blessing is for the man who will hear what God will do. Then let God do what He will do to glorify Himself.

This is the whole truth of the covenant of Abraham: God calling a man to Himself, then telling that man to walk with Him, promising him that if he would walk with Him in obedience, trusting in Him and following His guidance, he would be blessed. God would give the obedient believer everything he needed; and the believer like Abraham could know that what God would give him would be far more than what he could earn for himself. This end result of receiving the blessing of God and actually having the personal fellowship with God that is in the covenant with Abraham would not be reached by keeping rules and regulations; not by keeping the law, but by believing the promises of God.

To believe the promises of God one must know them, and this is one reason why Bible study is so very important. When thinking about the promises of Scripture we have in mind something in the New Testament that does not appear anywhere else. This is not the kind of thing the public knows about. The public may have ideas about standards of living, about what would be good and what wouldn't be good. People have a way of approving what they consider to be honorable and kind, and they often have a great deal of interest in doing the right and self-denying thing. They have many ideas along these lines, and they may teach them to one another if they want to; but none of this is what makes one a believer.

If a person were going to be a believer, he would have to yield himself in heart and mind and let the Holy Spirit work in him. He would need to leave Him alone to work in him; and the Holy Spirit, taking the things of Christ, would reveal them to him and strengthen him in it. This kind of living in Christ Jesus—being conscious of the presence of God so that a person is not alone but has God with him is a result not reached by keeping rules. The believer does not do everything so well that God will bless him: that is not the story. It is not that the believer is faithful in church attendance, in contributing to missions, and in all of the various things he would have to do to keep everything absolutely correct: that is not the way a person qualifies. All such things may be very fine: they can be very helpful; but there is no other qualification necessary beyond this: that one receives what God offers. If the believer appreciates it, so much the better; if he gives God thanks, so much the better; but everything must come from God. If a person wants to believe what God offers, he will need to be diligent in Bible study.

In this connection, in reading and studying the Bible, the believer would not have to read the Bible much, he would not have to study it much, to know that God is. The believer may need to learn something more about God, who is a rewarder of them that diligently seek Him; but the great facts of the gospel have been heard and are known. If the believer wants to understand them, reading them is one way that the Holy Spirit can use. And God can bless. If in his heart the believer is faithful to God as he reads and thinks about Him, the Holy Spirit will open his heart to enable him to believe about God.

When I accept Christ and receive Him, I will never be alone again; this is the blessing of Abraham. The Holy Spirit will be operative in me, and my mind will be guided into the will of God in the study of Scripture. When the Bible sounds exactly right to me and I can understand things in it, why is that? Because the Holy Spirit who is in *me* was in the men who wrote it. The Holy Spirit guided the writers. As the Spirit guided the writing, so the Holy Spirit guides the hearing. He will bless me as I listen, and He will strengthen me as I hear.

Here again is something I want to share with you: when you have yielded yourself to God, and when you have understood what Christ Jesus has done for you, and you have accepted it and turned to God, when all of this is done so that the Holy Spirit is operative in you, when you are conscious of the reality of God and of Jesus Christ, when you are aware that He died for you, that He rose again from the dead, when all these things are in your mind, they affect you in such a way that when you read the Bible, especially the New Testament, you will understand it. You will feel that it is something you know, you will feel that it is your own; and the reason you understand it, you are so familiar with it and feel you can use it is that the very One who inspired the writing of it, who was with the writers when they wrote it, is the very Holy Spirit who is in you now, in the reading of it. When we use the word "hearing"—by "the hearing of faith"—we mean Bible teaching and Bible preaching which we hear.

I hope that it will become clear to you that the blessing of Abraham, which is the promise of the Holy Spirit of God, will come to you as a free gift from God. You do not earn it; you do not qualify for it. You read it, you hear it, and you believe it. You receive it. God gives it to you. It is to His honor and glory. You will know well you did not do anything to earn it. You will know it was given to you as a gift. And this knowledge will fill you with gratitude and praise and thanksgiving; and these things are pleasing to God.

28

The Holy Spirit Is Given
to Each Believer as to a Son

Galatians 4:6

Did you know that every believer has the Holy Spirit in him? Not all believers realize the truth of the Holy Spirit; this is truly unfortunate. Many people who call themselves believers really do not understand about the Holy Spirit. No doubt many people are called believers and some even call themselves believers who really are *not* believers. This is not to say they couldn't be. Actually the Lord wants them to be; but so many people do not understand that. Many people think the word *Christian* is a cultural term, that if one acts in a certain way people will call him *Christian* because he is Christian-like.

Many people are called "Christian" by association. Their parents and brothers and sisters are believers; they go to Sunday School and church—maybe they are taken into the fellowship of believers and actually given that name. Many people begin to think that is all there is to being a Christian, but there is far more. There are many people called "Christians" who have never accepted Christ. It is sometimes shocking to find that many people are listed on the church rolls as members of the church who would frankly admit that they never were real believers and they have not ever given themselves over to walk in the ways of Christ. I think they possibly may some day expect to do so but I suspect that maybe the reason they have allowed their names to be put on the church roll is just because they would rather be counted "Christian" than "Mohammedan" or "Buddhist"; they would rather be counted as believers than to be thought of as not believing in God at all. Remember, no one can become a believer in himself; it is just not possible. One has to have personal dealings with Christ.

Let us turn now to Romans 8:9: "Now if any man have not the Spirit of Christ, he is none of his." That seems very plain, even blunt. Paul then goes on to argue:

And if Christ be in you, the body is dead because of sin; but the Spirit is life because of righteousness (Rom. 8:10).

If Christ be in you it is expected that the Holy Spirit will be in you.

But if the Spirit of him that raised up Jesus from the dead dwell in you, he that raised up Christ from the dead shall also quicken your mortal bodies by his Spirit that dwelleth in you (Rom. 8:11).

That is how it works by the Spirit that is within you. There is no such thing as being a Christian without that.

Therefore, brethren, we are debtors, not to the flesh, to live after the flesh. For if ye live after the flesh, ye shall die: but if ye through the Spirit do mortify the deeds of the body, ye shall live (Rom. 8:12-13).

There is no such thing as mortifying the deeds of the body in your own strength; that is never the idea. Some of you may try to do that; you actually try to control yourself and to mortify the deeds of the body and to put to death the human things in you in your own strength. You cannot do it; but the Holy Spirit in you can do it.

. . . but if ye through the Spirit do mortify the deeds of the body, ye shall live. For as many as are led by the Spirit of God, they are the sons of God (Rom. 8:13-14).

But so far as anyone is concerned, if you are a believer you will want to be sure that you have the benefits of belonging to Christ. There need be no question about it: when the Holy Spirit is operative in you, you will know it.

But when the fulness of the time was come, God sent forth his

Son, made of a woman, made under the law, To redeem them that were under the law, that we might receive the adoption of sons (Gal. 4:4-5).

That is what He sent Jesus Christ to do: "To redeem them that were under the law."

And because ye are sons, God hath sent forth the Spirit of his Son into your hearts, crying, Abba, Father (Gal. 4:6).

Despite the fact that verses 4 and 5 report "God sent forth His Son . . . to redeem them that were under the law," there will be a few people who will say, "All are redeemed." But this is not true. Only those who received Him were redeemed. Then God sent the Spirit of His Son into their hearts. Just as sinners need to receive the Lord Jesus Christ, so believers need to receive the Holy Spirit.

When the Holy Spirit is received into my heart, He moves me to have fellowship with the Father as a son, to feel toward God a closeness and a dependence upon Him as if He were actually my Father and I His son, which in truth is so. This is what makes communion with God precious; this is why communion with God is one of the greatest joys a Christian may ever have. When a Christian takes time to be conscious of the joy, to pray and sing praises to God, and to give testimony, his heart is filled with gladness.

Herein lies the strength for obedience in conduct. While we have been showing forth certain things that are taught about the Holy Spirit I hope the idea has been growing in your mind that in the whole Christian life God works in you. "For it is God which worketh in you both to will and to do of his good pleasure" (Phil. 2:13). God holds up the believer. Being a believer is not a matter of outward conduct. Some will even emphasize that while they may not show the work of the Spirit outwardly, the truth is still that the Holy Spirit working in them will bring things to pass. This is the remarkable work of the Holy Spirit, given to be with each believer, inclining him to look to God as Father and to have fellowship and communion with Him.

29

The Child of God
Is "Born After the Spirit"

Galatians 4:29

Do you realize that the spiritual life of a Christian is entirely different and separate from his physical life? Paul implies this when he writes:

> But as then he that was born after the flesh persecuted him that was born after the Spirit, even so it is now (Gal. 4:29).

Here he distinguishes two classes of people: one born after the flesh, another born after the Spirit. This distinction is to be seen all through Scripture.

The word *flesh* includes everything that is natural or human, and the word *Spirit* refers to everything that is in Christ Jesus, that is revealed to us by the Spirit, and that comes out of the will of the living God. In the universe as a whole there is a difference between the Creator and the creation. Just how big the Creator is we have no way of estimating, except to say that He is as big as anything He made. We speak of Him as being Almighty. And the creation—the universe—includes everything that is—far beyond anything we can see or hear or sense in any way.

When we speak of the visible world which we can see, we could also speak of the audible world which we can hear and the tangible world which we can touch. There is another world—the invisible world. We can't touch it, hear it, see it, taste it, or smell it. That is where the power of God is. The difference is to be recognized, and the Lord Jesus made use of it when He said, "What shall it profit a man if he gain the whole world" (the visible world) "and lose his own soul?" (the invisible world).

To understand this distinction, think of a person who is a man in his home, while at the same time he may be a doctor. He would have some distinctive characteristics because he is a doctor but at the same time he would have the general characteristics of a man. The difference in these aspects is also to be seen and felt in the case of Cain and Abel. These men were brothers. They had the same father and mother, yet they were so different. We can think that Cain was of the flesh and Abel was of the Spirit. Cain did things that were pleasing to himself; Abel did things that were pleasing to God.

Abraham had two sons: Ishmael and Isaac. Ishmael is thought of as a son of the flesh, whereas Isaac is spoken of as the son of promise—a child of the Spirit. So with Isaac's children: he had twins—Esau and Jacob. Esau is referred to as being of the flesh, and Jacob was a man who ultimately had his name changed to Israel, and who became a mighty man of God. In general, this distinction is discernible in our day when we consider a person as a human being or as a child of God. The difference shows up in conduct, of course. The human being acts in a way that suits himself; the child of God acts in a way that pleases God. This difference in conduct is not always absolute because a human being can pretend to be a child of God, and a child of God on occasion may fall into old habits that are quite human; but there is a distinct difference in origin.

When a man and woman come together as husband and wife in the flesh, and become the parents of a child, we speak of that as the first birth. Then we recognize that, as the Lord Jesus said in the third chapter of John, a person can be born again; in fact, "you must be born again." This new beginning takes place between the soul and God. It is made possible by the Word of God and activated by the Holy Spirit of God. When a person receives the Word of God into his heart and believes it, God produces something in that person that is new: he is now a new creature in Christ Jesus. Everyone who is born again is a new creation, old things are passed away, and behold all things are become new. The human being responds to the physical, and in his feelings he is affected by what goes on around him, by the natural physical world in which he lives; but the born-again believer responds to the spiritual and is affected by the promises of God, by the Word of God and by fellowship with God.

In I John 2:16 it is written that the natural man is concerned with "the lust of the flesh, the lust of the eyes and the pride of life." He may be civilized, even cultured, but it is still true that as a natural man he is thinking of himself. The spiritually-minded person wishes to be well pleasing in the sight of the Lord, finding his satisfaction and joy in the Lord. Paul says it is always true that the person who lives naturally will persecute the person who lives spiritually. No doubt this is true partly because the human being tends to be arrogant, to push himself, while the spiritual person is inclined to be meek, seeking only that which is pleasing to God. When the Holy Spirit is active and operative in him, a person will be inclined to do the will of God. He may expect to find persecution in this world, but he will have joy in the Lord.

30

The Believer Awaits Righteousness "Through the Spirit"

Galatians 5:5

Did you know that an intelligent believer waits for the Lord to produce righteousness in him?

For we through the Spirit wait for the hope of righteousness by faith (Gal. 5:5).

These words were written by Paul to the Galatians by way of explaining to them certain things that were true about their living in faith. Here he is saying, "For we [believers] through the Spirit [by the indwelling Holy Spirit of God and by the guidance that He gives us] wait for the hope of righteousness by faith."

Believers are concerned about their conduct just as all men are. A baseball pitcher would like to pitch well, a man who paints the house wants to paint it well. Believers in Christ want to do right. Naturally! I should perhaps say spiritually, because the Holy Spirit within shows them the things of Christ. One of the frustrations of man is his inability to always do right when he wants to. "For that which I do I allow not: for what I would, that do I not; but what I hate, that do I. . . . For the good that I would I do not: but the evil which I would not, that I do" (Rom. 7:15, 19).

Something we are inclined to forget is that the believer in himself is no stronger than other people are in themselves. So far as the individual human being is concerned, when he becomes a believer one of the biggest mistakes he could make would be to imagine that he has become an angel. Everybody else will know it first, and sooner or later he will find out that he is no angel.

Suppose several men walking across the country get mired in a swamp. Now they would be floundering around and would be in great danger of sinking out of sight. Then suppose one of them finds a rock and stands on it. He would not be sinking anymore. The others would still be sinking. Now consider this man standing on the rock and think about the others round about him who are still sinking in the sand: is this man standing on the rock safe because he is so strong? No. The rock is solid; that is why he is safe.

The same truth can be seen in the case of eight men who are on a sinking ship and are thrown into the water. Suppose a lifeboat picks up five of the men but three of them cannot be found. If those three men drown and the five escape, is it because the five are better swimmers? No! They may not even be swimming: they are safe because they are in the lifeboat. This is how it is with a believer: when he comes to the Lord Jesus Christ he will be safe.

There is always the temptation for the believer to try to do right in his own strength. The members of the Galatian church in the days of Paul were trying to do this by keeping regulations. After they became believers well-meaning people told them the way to live a good life was to obey the law of Moses and to live by rules. The rules in themselves and the law of Moses are not bad, but keeping them is not the basis of the righteousness of a person who believes in the Lord Jesus Christ. Christ's righteousness is imputed to the believer, who is accepted as righteous in the sight of God.

The interesting thing is that when sinners are reconciled to God in this fashion, so there is nothing against them on the books, they are given free entrance into the presence of God and something happens to their spirits. They become profoundly grateful and are anxious to please God. The believer will be kept by the power of God and the righteousness of God will be actually produced in him by the work of the Holy Spirit within his soul. This is what Paul meant when he wrote: "We through the Spirit wait for the hope of righteousness by faith." Paul is saying that as believers we wait for the expectation that we will be everything we ought to be, and we wait for this by faith.

Waiting does not imply being inactive; waiting isn't a case of sitting down in a rocking chair, of being lazy or presumptuous. When a believer is waiting on the Lord, he is not standing still or sleeping on the job. He does what the Lord wants him to do and waits for the results; he yields the way Christ leads him to yield, and waits for His help. In worship he recalls what Christ has done for him. A farmer waiting for the harvest has more to do than just wait all summer long for harvesttime to come and then reap a crop. He plants the field and puts in the crop, he then watches over it and nurtures it until harvesttime, that he might get from the harvest according to what he put in and the way he cared for it during the growing season.

I can trust in the Lord, yield myself to Him, and this will be waiting for the hope of righteousness by faith. When I am exercising faith and believing in Christ I will be obeying, serving, and doing all that is to be expected of me. If I am to wait by faith, faith is not a matter of just standing still. James said that faith without works is dead, and that is the situation here. If I believe in the Lord Jesus Christ and receive Him into my heart so that the Holy Spirit comes to me, I am moved into the will of the Lord Jesus Christ, expecting consequences to follow. Thus obeying is an essential part of believing and this is done in waiting.

The will of the Lord Jesus Christ in me will be to do right; I will do the right thing and this will show up in my conduct as a result of obedience. So the believer awaits righteousness to appear in himself through the Spirit. It is the Spirit of God who makes this waiting possible as He activates this response in the heart and experience of the believer.

31

The Holy Spirit Is Contrary to the Flesh

Galatians 5:16-17

Can you understand how it is that a believer has a sort of civil war going on inside himself?

This I say then, Walk in the Spirit, and ye shall not fulfil the lust of the flesh. For the flesh lusteth against the Spirit, and the Spirit against the flesh: and these are contrary the one to the other: so that ye cannot do the things that ye would (Gal. 5:16-17).

Thus the apostle Paul described a sort of continuing battle, a civil war between the flesh, which is definitely at home in this world, and the Spirit that has definitely moved into his heart. A person is born naturally as a human being and all that he has in himself is called "flesh"; but he is born again by the Spirit and the Word of God, and everything he has in Christ Jesus is called "Spirit." These two are contrary the one to the other; "the flesh lusteth against the Spirit, and the Spirit lusteth against the flesh." This is the situation about which Paul gives very simple but very profound advice: "Walk in the Spirit, and ye shall not fulfil the lust of the flesh." This is the clue to practical, sure deliverance for the believer.

Many years ago it was my privilege to serve in the Canadian Army as a training instructor. One morning when I was supposed to be on parade at 8:00, the sergeant in charge called us to order at 7:55. Later in the day, because I was minded to be precise about things, I took the matter up with the sergeant. I said, "According to my watch it was five minutes to eight when you called the roll this morning. If I had not been there at 7:55 would you have marked me late?" He turned to me in a patient way (the way one deals with a child) and said, "It has been established here in the Army that if a man is five minutes early he will never be late." Throughout all the years I have never forgotten that bit of learning. Think about it. Five minutes early: you will never be late. If you want to avoid doing wrong, do right.

Walk in the Spirit and you will not succumb to the lust of the flesh. Paul was writing about this in Ephesians when he was talking about putting off the old man and putting on the new man. He also admonished the believers not to lie one to another but to speak the truth every man to his neighbor. He urged them to start moving in the direction in which the Spirit led. In the original language the word *lust* means strong desire, and the way of escape for the believer is to move in the way in which the Spirit moves, which is to do the will of God, to be well pleasing in His sight.

Every now and again I meet believers who seem to feel proud because they have moved from the way of wickedness to the way of righteousness. Yet they seem to lag, to drag their feet as though they were in a funeral march. That is not the way to do it! When the believer has a strong desire to do right, he should move with vigor and joy in the direction of that which is right; because the flesh has a strong desire to do evil and it will move fast in that other direction. Because the flesh lusteth against the Spirit and the Spirit against the

104

flesh and these are contrary one to the other, victory and triumph will result from prompt vigorous action.

When I was in the Philippines a minister asked, "If a person has in him the spirit of the flesh, which is to do evil, and also the Spirit of Christ, which is to do right, how can these two be in the same man?" I had that day been watching the plowing of a rice field where a big water buffalo was used for power. This water buffalo was being ridden and guided by a little boy. I drew attention to the fact that when I saw the big water buffalo and the little boy I noted that "These two are contrary one to the other. The buffalo wants to do one thing and the little boy wants to do another." Then I pointed out that as long as the little boy rides on top there is peaceful coexistence; but should the buffalo be on top and the boy on the bottom, there would be trouble. I then went on to note that that is the way it is with the flesh and the Spirit: if the Spirit controls the flesh there is peaceful coexistence, but if the flesh is in control, there is trouble. The flesh everyone has; we are all born with it; the Spirit is given by God to us when we are willing to believe in Christ.

Be thankful, give God the praise, and you will not grumble. Be kind and gentle, and you will not be harsh or hard. The Holy Spirit will help the believer along this line. If you walk in the Spirit, you will not fulfill the desires of the flesh.

32

Walking in the Spirit Is Normal for One Who Lives in the Spirit

Galatians 5:25

Have you ever imagined what would happen if believers would all live according to what they believe?

If we live in the Spirit, let us also walk in the Spirit (Gal. 5:25).

In this simple statement by the apostle Paul the word "if" is not so much a question as it is a condition. Believers could say to one another: "Since we live spiritually in the Spirit, affected by the Spirit of God, and since that is what we count on for our spiritual nourishment, let us also walk in the Spirit, let us play it that way."

Believers are probably as sincere as anyone else, yet they still may be foolish enough to overlook the great privilege they have in being the children of God. It is a very common thing among mankind to hold certain things to be true and then not live by them. Young people going to school naturally are anxious about their grades; they know that if they would do their work carefully, they could be well off: yet even though they are in high school—or perhaps in college— they actually will let their work go undone. This is a snare any person may fall into.

This is equally true in spiritual matters. To be blessed of God includes not only forgiveness when I do wrong and cleansing when I have sinned, but it also includes guidance for tomorrow. I could be given strength for the day. A believer need not wait until afterward to confess his mistake and to receive forgiveness; he could ask the Lord beforehand and be led into that which is good, and be endued with power to accomplish the will of God. But it is a common mistake that often we talk instead of walk. It is such a temptation to talk a great game, but not to play it; and this is tragic. Throughout the Book of Galatians, Paul has been saying that our spiritual life, which is of the Lord Jesus Christ, does not come to us by any efforts of our own; it is what God will give to us. God has given His Holy Spirit to lead and to guide the believers. And since we live in the Spirit, and God has blessed us in the Spirit, let us also walk in the Spirit.

There are a number of ways in which we can see how this will work. The Spirit, for instance, will show the soul that God is; God is everywhere and over all, God is a rewarder. Inasmuch as the Spirit shows these things to the believer, the believer will put God first. This means he will put God before his family, his business, his pleasure, and before his own personal ideas. He will be conscious of God. He will not do this because he is asked to do so or because he is afraid to do anything else. He will do this because it is a privilege. The Spirit will show him that God is a rewarder of them that diligently seek Him. The Spirit will also show him that the soul is more important than the body.

Since all this is true, the believer will seek first the Kingdom of God and let all other things be added to it. And that means when he is making his plans—all of them—he avoids thinking in terms of what he is going to get out of them in this world's goods. He will think rather in terms of what would be pleasing in the sight of God. He will have this in mind as he goes about his affairs every day. The Spirit will show him that the soul is more important than the body and that he should keep this in mind.

Another spiritual truth is that Christ died for our sins. When we say that Christ died for our sins, how many do we mean? All! Then if He died for our sins, how many will we suffer for? None! I am to understand His death covers all our sins. If we really believe that Christ died for our sins then let us make it a point to believe this in our case and rid ourselves of any feeling of guilt, of being unacceptable in the sight of God. This is what the Holy Spirit will show us: that God sent forth His Son, who died for our sins, and the Holy Spirit to be given to believers. Inasmuch as that is the case, then let us walk that way; let us yield to Him moment by moment.

Whenever I am faced with a situation and I have a moment of prayer, I should stop and listen inside my own soul to understand how I am being led from within. I remember meeting a believer recently who had just been called into an important responsibility. She was a woman with a task to perform for which she did not feel at all adequate. When I talked with her about it and praised her for what she was doing, she told me, "Oh, *I* couldn't do it. I have no idea what each day will bring forth in my job, but I am trusting the Lord moment by moment. He carries it, not I." This woman understood this great truth and she let the Lord carry the load; all she did was obey Him.

Another truth that the Holy Spirit will bring to the mind of the believer is that God in providence is over all. The Holy Spirit will show this. Then let the believer walk in the Spirit, putting away care and anxiety, fearfulness and dread, uneasiness and unbelief. If God is over all, the believer can be absolutely sure that what happens is God's will. In this connection the Holy Spirit will assure him that whatever happens is known to God. If it is good, God knows it; and if it is bad, God knows it. This being the case, then let us say with Job: "The Lord hath given; the Lord hath taken away. Blessed be the name of the Lord." To be able to do this in every way is walking in the Spirit.

"In quietness and confidence shall be thy strength." These are the words that are brought to the heart by the Holy Spirit of God. The believer does not have to make Him do it; God will do this for all believers. The Holy Spirit will show believers the things of God. Paul would exhort us as believers: "Let us walk in them."

33

Sowing to the Spirit Brings the Harvest of Life Everlasting

Galatians 6:7-8

Do you realize that if a man wants the life of God in his own experience he can arrange for that in a simple, reasonable way?

Be not deceived; God is not mocked: for whatsoever a man soweth, that shall he also reap. For he that soweth to his flesh shall of the flesh reap corruption; but he that soweth to the Spirit shall of the Spirit reap life everlasting (Gal. 6:7-8).

This is a common truth widely known: "Whatsoever a man soweth, that shall he also reap." Nobody in the world will have a question about that; all know it to be true. It is also just about as common for everyone to feel that this is a warning. But why should it not likewise be taken as a promise? The fact is that it is so commonly taken as a warning because the common reaction actually reflects the common sense of guilt.

Most of us do the things that please ourselves; and so, when I call to mind "Whatsoever a man soweth, that shall he also reap," I know right away I have been doing the things that please myself; therefore, I can expect that kind of result. But believers can remember the other side of that truth. There is a promise here, "Whatsoever a man soweth, that shall he also reap." The believer is led to sow to the Spirit, for of the Spirit he shall reap life everlasting. No doubt there is much lost by this oversight when it is forgotten that this truth has in it great promise.

Years ago, when I first came into the part of the country where I now live I heard with much appreciation various Negro spiritual songs. On one occasion I heard a song with many verses that had one particular refrain that was repeated over and over: "You're a-gonna reap just what you sow." The last stanza had a message I have never forgotten. It went something like this, "You tell that mother to keep on a-prayin'; she's a-gonna reap just what she sows." Through the years that song has often come to mind as a great promise. I have seen it waving in the breeze, so to speak, on the horizon of my consciousness; I have looked upon it as a flag up on a flagpole. Isn't it wonderful to know that if you sow to the Spirit (and you can) you shall of the Spirit reap life everlasting? That is the promise of God.

How would a person sow to the Spirit? By doing what the Spirit leads one to do. One of the first things the Holy Spirit prompts a soul to do is to worship God. He will turn your heart and mind to God so that in your private life, in your going about your work, you will remember God. The Holy Spirit will show the things of God, and you will worship Him, think about Him, pray to Him, bring things before Him, and ask His guidance. You will do this in public, you will go to church, you will seek fellowship with other believers. You will hear an announcement about special services at the church, and you will make your plans to attend. In other words, you will be ready to worship God at all times, because the Spirit will show you these things. If you will worship God and draw nigh to God, He will bless you and He will draw nigh to you. He is a living being and if you worship Him He has ways of blessing you.

Then again, if you want to sow to the Spirit there is one thing the Holy Spirit will lead you to do, and that is to read the Bible. You will not only read the Bible, you will study it. In the average community there are Bible study groups. You will join one. The Holy Spirit will lead you to do this, and God will bless you.

If you are following the guidance of the Holy Spirit, He will prompt you to pray to God in a personal and in an intimate fashion. You will take everything to God in prayer. Maybe you are worrying about things, then the Spirit will prompt you to talk to God. When you are making plans for the day, you will take this to God in prayer and He will bless you. If you have a family, the Holy Spirit will lead you to pray together. You will together seek the blessing of God.

110

You will study the Bible together and God will bless you. The Holy Spirit will lead you in the matter of public prayer and in personal praying. As surely as you pray, God will bless you. If you sow to the Spirit you shall of the Spirit reap life everlasting.

There is one other thing I should like to urge that you do in the matter of following the Spirit: witness for the Lord. Tell others about Him. Let it be known that you care about the souls of other people—that you are interested in turning them to God if at all possible. This is something else the Spirit will lead you to do. And remember, "He that soweth to the Spirit shall of the Spirit reap life everlasting." And so, if you want the favor of God—the life of God in daily experience—it can be arranged. It is only necessary simply to do what the Spirit leads you to do; yield yourself to God and He will bless you, to the glory of His Name.

34

The Holy Spirit Is
"The Earnest of our Inheritance"

Ephesians 1:13-14

Did you know there is one aspect of the experience of a believer here on earth that will not be changed in heaven?

The apostle Paul wrote thus to the believers in Ephesus:

In whom ye also trusted, after that ye heard the word of truth, the gospel of your salvation: in whom also after that ye believed, ye were sealed with that holy Spirit of promise,

Which is the earnest of our inheritance until the redemption of the purchased possession, unto the praise of his glory (Eph. 1:13-14).

As we look at this we will see a number of words used that belong to the financial world; they have to do with the buying and selling of property. For instance, when two people make a trade the bargain must be sealed; and spiritually speaking, we are sealed with the Holy Spirit of promise: the agreement is real and it will not be broken. In the business world when a trade is made, often a part of the price is paid in the beginning; this is called "earnest money." When the believer accepts Christ Jesus the agreement to save the soul is sealed when he receives the Holy Spirit, "which is the earnest of our inheritance."

When a person accepts the Lord Jesus Christ, what happens is that he gives himself over to God in order that he may receive Christ. When the blessing that comes with the Lord Jesus Christ is received, he will have everything in the future that we commonly call heaven. The believer does have a future, not only here and now in his earthly life because God takes care of and helps him, but there and forever in heaven. Paul calls that future "our inheritance." You and I would commonly call it heaven. It can be thought of as an inheritance, because the believer does not earn it. When my father died I received a certain amount of money. Since I didn't earn it, that money was my inheritance. It was given to me. This is the way we are to understand the blessing of God in Christ Jesus: not earned, not bought, but received from God as a gift.

We can also think of our blessing in Christ as an inheritance because an inheritance is usually received after the death of the donor. Believers are spoken of as being the heirs of God—joint heirs with Jesus Christ. It is common to speak about heaven and its blessing as being the inheritance that believers have. In all such thinking it should be kept in mind that the one person who died, who made it possible for believers to have this inheritance, was none other than the Lord Jesus Christ. When He died for us He made available to us His legacy, so to speak, and through Him we received the inheritance of the Lord Jesus Christ from Almighty God.

Part of that free gift that we receive, and that we commonly speak of as heaven, is the Holy Spirit in the heart. What the Holy Spirit in the heart actually does is to show us the things of Jesus Christ. This reality of having the Holy Spirit of God in me, making me aware of the Lord Jesus Christ, will never be changed; this is going to be the same in heaven as it is here.

The one bit of heaven we have in this world is the personal fellowship with Almighty God through His Holy Spirit when we are together with the Lord Jesus Christ as head and we as members of His body. When we are together as bride and bridegroom, the Holy Spirit shows us the things of Christ and inclines our hearts toward Him. Thus we are sealed with that Holy Spirit which is promised to us—the earnest of our inheritance—until the redemption of the purchased possession, unto the praise of His glory.

We speak of the redemption of a piece of property that had a mortgage on it as "paying off the mortgage." You and I as human beings were guilty of sin and we were under condemnation. "The soul that sinneth it shall die." The prospect was that as sinners we would be doomed to death, banished from the presence of God. This doom that was before us was like a mortgage. This would have to be removed or we would be destroyed; this is the state of being lost. When Christ Jesus died for us, He paid that mortgage: He redeemed our souls. A token of this grace, a down payment of this mercy, is the Holy Spirit. This is the way for you and for me to have a new appreciation of the significance of the fellowship of the Lord Jesus Christ, while we are still on earth. When we get to heaven we shall see Him as He is.

35

All Believers Are Builded Together Through the Spirit

Ephesians 2:19-22

Do you understand how it is possible for all believers, as different as they are, to be together in one fellowship? Paul writes to the Ephesian believers about the fellowship of believers in Christ, and how they are all blended together in one communion.

Now therefore ye are no more strangers and foreigners, but fellowcitizens with the saints, and of the household of God; And are built upon the foundation of the apostles and prophets, Jesus Christ himself being the chief corner stone; In whom all the building fitly framed together groweth unto an holy temple in the Lord: In whom ye also are builded together for an habitation of God through the Spirit (Eph. 2:19-22).

We should emphasize that last phrase, because through the functioning of the Holy Spirit within, all believers are built together as a dwelling place for God. We need to think about the great work of the Holy Spirit in helping believers to live the life of faith. Scripture shows plainly that the gospel teaches that the Holy Spirit is given to the church. In order that believers may live together in their unity the Holy Spirit is actively operative in each and builds them all together for a habitation of God through the Spirit.

It is a great truth in the revelation that God dwells in His people. The Bible teaches that not only is the church the temple of the living God, but the body of the believer is the temple of the Holy Spirit. Just now the focus of attention is on the church and the fact that God dwells among His people in the fellowship of His people.

In the time of Moses the place of worship was a tabernacle, and in that structure the people came face to face with God through the

High Priest. It was directed that whenever the people settled down and took up their places to establish camp, they should arrange their twelve tribes in such a way that in the center of the camp was the tabernacle. There would be three tribes to the north, three to the east, three to the south, and three to the west. In this way it was impressed on the mind and the heart of everybody that the house of God was the real center for the people, and thus His presence would be in the very midst of them.

This had a profound effect upon the Israelites. They were told that they would have to be holy in their conduct because God was holy in His nature. This was the inspiration for some very specific and effective rules and regulations of sanitation and hygiene. Things were done because of those regulations that students of health today say were very effective methods of sanitation and hygiene. The people were to be clean since God was in their midst and God was holy. He said to the people, "Be ye holy for I am holy." Being holy meant that there was to be no wickedness, no defilement among them.

In many symbols and events in the Old Testament the truth was brought out to the people that God was with His people. In one place He is spoken of as "Emmanuel," which in the Hebrew means "God with us." In the Book of Ephesians Paul uses the figure of the temple to point out that believers are builded together into a holy temple for the habitation of God—a place for God to stay. In I Corinthians it is distinctly said that the church is the temple of the living God. Peter, in his first epistle, speaks of "lively stones built up in a spiritual house." Paul states in Ephesians, "In whom all the building fitly framed together groweth unto an holy temple in the Lord." Paul is emphasizing here the idea that all the Christians taken together constitute an arrangement where God can be in their midst. The figure of speech is a bit forced when we talk about the temple here, because it speaks of the temple growing. A temple doesn't grow, but in this case it did because it was the growing of the body of Christ. The temple brings out the idea that God was in them. While the figure of speech is somewhat forced, the truth is clear. All believers are builded together for a habitation of God through the

Spirit; this is the New Testament reality which was promised in Old Testament Scripture.

The temple was built of stone, and before that the tabernacle had been made of skins, but the true temple of God is not made of the skins of animals, and it is not made of stone or wood; it is made of the hearts and minds of believers. They are so coordinated that they can be used as one unit and one plan can be performed through them. The parts of the body of Christ are all different but they are used as one unit.

Let us think about any church building. It has doorways, but is all the wall a door? No! Much of the wall is made of brick or stone, but there are doorways and there are windows. Is all the wall a window? No! Not all the wall is a window. Then there is a roof, but is the whole church a roof? No! Then there is a floor. Is the whole church a floor? No! But the church building has a floor, a door, walls, windows, roof, and foundation, and inside the building there are pews. This place where the people come together to worship has various items in it, but it is spoken of as the dwelling place of God.

Just as there are these parts of the building, so it is with the church. Many different members are in it, and each has his place. Some teach, some pray, some give, and some govern. The parts of the body of Christ, like the members of one's body, are all different in themselves, yet they operate together into one.

The human hand is no doubt one of the most wonderful structures in the physical world. The hand has many bones, many joints with sinews and nerves and muscles, and with structures such as the thumb and the four fingers. Each is different; each is set in a different place, yet blending together, working together, they make one hand. If all fingers did the same thing, there would not be a hand; there would be a flipper.

The members of the church are like the fingers of the hand. Each finger is separated from the other, each acts according to its own responsibility and function, but together they act as a hand. So it is with the church—each believer has a share. All of those who are in Christ Jesus belong in the church. They differ from one another, just as the thumb differs from the little finger; but they cooperate and they are coordinated in such a way that they work together as one unit. This unity is accomplished by the Holy Spirit of God: believers are builded together for a habitation of God. Each believer can participate in the things of the Lord as he follows the guidance of the Spirit. May the Lord help us to understand this, so that we may have an attitude toward others of appreciating them in their function and their place.

36

The Spirit Reveals Truth in the Gospel to Apostles and Prophets

Ephesians 3:5-6

Have you ever wondered how the apostles and prophets came to know the Word of God? When the apostle Paul was writing to the believers at Ephesus, he wrote about his own ministry among them, how it was his privilege to preach certain truths to them which had not previously been known. In this connection he says:

Which in other ages was not made known unto the sons of men, as it is now revealed unto his holy apostles and prophets by the Spirit (Eph. 3:5).

Much is implied in this short statement.

Here are some important ideas that you and I can look at with profit. You will notice that not all truth is revealed at all times, or for that matter at any one time. The apostle Paul could say that there was certain truth revealed now that had not been revealed before and this was a fact that research could never discover. When we speak about the revelation of some truth of God or of the Word of God, many people will want to compare that to the kind of discovery of truth that occurs when one uses a telescope, a microscope, or a surveyor's chain. But these are two different kinds of truth altogether.

There is a type of truth that has to do with the description of things—something is so long, so wide, so deep, or it weighs so much. That is the kind of thing that can be measured; or, if something happened at a certain time, the kind of thing that can be reported. If something exists in a certain place—even if it is out of sight—it is there and you can believe it; it actually exists. These are items of fact.

But this is not the kind of truth that Paul was referring to. There are items of fact, things that have to do with external reality; but there is also spiritual truth, things that have to do with inner spiritual reality. For instance, there are some things that research cannot discover. For example, who knows what your own plans for the future are? There is no way that anybody could figure out what you are going to do tomorrow because when the time comes you might turn to the right or you might turn to the left, in the exercise of a freedom which is part of our human equipment.

The spiritual truth that is in the Word of God is like that; it is not the description of anything or arrangement, but it is an announcement of intention. It is something that God will do. This has not been finished as yet; much of this is for the future. Because the promises are intentions we say they are inscrutable, that is, one cannot see them. God knows what He will do and when He will do it, but He has not revealed that to anyone. So it can be said that so far as the truth of God's will is concerned, not all is revealed at any time; only as much as God wants to reveal.

When Scripture says "which in other ages was not made known," it is apparent all ages of history are not alike. Even in the revelation of God there is a progression. Things move in their course: first the blade, then the ear, then the full corn in the ear. The new revelation that comes from time to time never contradicts the old. Some truth was already known. The new truth may change the situation, and it may change the particular action and treatment at the time, but it will not be found contradictory.

It is possible that certain things are revealed today that the people of God in the time of Moses and David did not know. These are equally authentic as the Word of God. The present age is fortunate in having the fuller revelation. Paul writes, "Which in other ages was not made known unto the sons of men, as it is now revealed."

Apostles and prophets are active now. Both classes of servants, apostles and prophets, have to do with preaching and teaching the Word of God. Generally speaking, the word *apostle* refers to somebody who can interpret with authority, who can give the real meaning that God had in mind when a particular thing was done; and a prophet is one who faithfully preaches what has been interpreted. Any one man might be both an apostle and a prophet since he might function in each of these two different ways.

Holy apostles and prophets had truth revealed to them. The word *holy* refers primarily to the fact that they were committed, genuinely sincere men. This suggests that God's revelation will be to men who are totally committed. The truth that was revealed unto these men was not arrived at by research or experimentation on their part. This is not the kind of truth that can be discovered by examination. Nor did a group of men get together to figure out what God would say; God Himself revealed His truth to His holy apostles and prophets.

Today much emphasis is given to a certain aspect of education. Much attention is given to a "buzz session," on the basis that the way to arrive at truth is by having a general talk-around. But that is *not* the way *this* truth was revealed! Holy apostles and prophets did not arrive at this truth while in conference or in consultation among themselves. This was revelation that God gave to certain chosen men who were especially qualified. It was not that they were unusually good or smart, but they were "gifted," spiritually speaking. They were given the capacity to understand the will of God, so they could receive this revelation. These apostles and prophets, then, by explaining and preaching would convey to the people what the mind of God was.

The fact is that the Holy Spirit reveals truth in the gospel through chosen men of God: apostles and prophets who share it with other people.

37

The Holy Spirit Strengthens a Believer to Believe Christ Dwells in Him

Ephesians 3:16-17

Do you realize that it takes spiritual strength to believe the indwelling Christ? The apostle Paul wrote to the Ephesian believers:

That he would grant you, according to the riches of his glory,
to be strengthened with might by his Spirit in the inner man;
That Christ may dwell in your hearts by faith (Eph. 3:16-17).

Paul is praying that believers should be enabled to grasp this truth. This very important fact is often not realized: it takes spiritual strength to believe the truth about the indwelling Christ.

It is possible to be so weak spiritually that a person cannot believe. Spiritual truth is something that is revealed by the Holy Spirit of God. When a soul is influenced by the Holy Spirit of God, such capacity is not received personally or naturally; it is not that the person has a trusting disposition or a strong will. Certain things are revealed in the gospel about Jesus Christ. These things when heard profoundly affect the soul. This is the work of the Holy Spirit. Truths about Jesus Christ are brought to mind as the believer reads them in the Bible or as he hears them when they are being preached. The Holy Spirit impresses them upon the soul and strengthens that soul from within to accept these things.

The Holy Spirit shows such truth about the Lord Jesus Christ that the soul will find it easy to believe in Him. This, then, is the work of the Holy Spirit. Much of such truth is usually about factual data; because the soul would like to know what things look like and what has happened: such data as can be discovered in research or have been set forth by logic. But spiritual truth—the operation in you of the Holy Spirit of God—is grounded in the will and purpose of God. A person hears the things of Christ: believing them is taking them to be true. The question is, will you take them to be true? Can you believe them? Will you commit yourself to them?

The confidence to do this is produced in you by the operation of the Holy Spirit, showing you the things of the Lord Jesus Christ. The truth that Paul refers to is a truth that cannot be sensed—it is revealed. The Word of God is spoken to us. That requires on our part, hearing the Word, understanding it, and believing it. This requires strength.

There is an element of volition in faith. If you are waiting until you are convinced absolutely as if somebody were forcing you to believe, don't be surprised if you never believe. One element of faith is that you must of yourself rise up and take what God has offered to you. The strength to do this is called grace, and you will need a certain amount of grace to believe.

Some years ago a famous philosopher in America wrote an essay entitled "The Will to Believe." It emphasized a very important line of truth. If Christ is to be received in my heart I will have to take Him as I heard He was presented to me. Christ dwells in me: that means that He collaborates with me and I with Him. We work together in attitude and in faith; we work together in obedience to God and in patience. And since Christ dwells in my heart, He moves me to a certain response to the Father.

Believing is an action on the part of a person; it is a matter of

121

keeping some Word of God in mind and yielding to and obeying Him. This requires strength—the strength of conviction and commitment. And this strength of conviction is produced by the Holy Spirit of God, who shows me the things of Christ and makes them vivid to me.

Apparently the coming of the Spirit into the heart is a work of God because Paul could pray for it. He prayed that "God would grant that you might be strengthened with might by His Spirit in the inner man [so that you can believe] that Christ may dwell in your heart by faith."

38

The Holy Spirit Leads a Believer Beyond the Law

Galatians 5:18

Would you know how a Christian could avoid doing wrong?

But if ye be led of the Spirit, ye are not under the law (Gal. 5:18).

These words seem very simple, yet the truth is so profound it would be easy to miss their meaning.

In considering the truth of the Holy Spirit, we do not think about what He looks like. It would be very difficult to describe a sunbeam or to describe the sweet perfume of a rose. Such things can be seen and sensed, but the Holy Spirit is invisible: it is impossible to sense

Him in any way. But there is a way to think about Him: one can notice what He does and how He affects the individual believer.

We know who He is; He is the third person in the Godhead: God, the Father; God, the Son; God, the Holy Spirit. We know, too, that He has come to dwell in the hearts of believers. From the day of Pentecost the Holy Spirit has been dwelling in the hearts of believers here in this world. We know, too, that He shows the things of Christ to the individual believer. As the Holy Spirit is doing this work, the believer becomes aware of the Lord Jesus Christ, so that he has with him at all times the conscious presence of the Lord Jesus Christ. This is the result of the work of the Holy Spirit. In His place in the heart, He shows the things of Christ.

The things of Christ are to be seen in what Jesus of Nazareth did. Christ Jesus died on Calvary's cross for sinners. He was buried. He really went into death and stayed there three days. He arose from the dead, gloriously, triumphantly. He is now in the presence of God, and He has sent forth His Holy Spirit into our hearts. The presence of God is with us, while Christ Jesus is waiting now for us and watching over us.

I remember one time I had an experience which could have been very annoying and irritating, but just at that moment there came into my mind a very clear picture of the dying Jesus Christ on the cross, and the thought that though He was reviled, He reviled not again; though He was falsely accused, He answered never a word. These things came to my mind so vividly that they hushed my soul. I did not have a word to say; I was being affected by the Holy Spirit of God. In this way He inclines the heart and the will into obedience to the will of Christ. This is the work of the Holy Spirit. If I am led by the Spirit, He shows me the things of Christ and affects me in such a way that I am moved into yielding myself to Him: then something happens to me such as happened to the Lord Jesus Christ in Gethsemane. There, looking up into the face of His Father, He said, "O my Father, if it be possible, let this cup pass from me: nevertheless not as I will, but as thou wilt" (Matt. 26:39). If I have the Holy Spirit in my soul, He will show me the things of Christ; there will be meekness and I will hold no grudge against anybody. I will look upon others with compassion. Why? Because the Spirit of Christ is in my heart.

Paul would say against such there is no law. The law was given for evildoers. For instance, if the speed limit were fifty miles per hour, and you were driving along at forty-five miles an hour, there could be a policeman stationed at every corner and it wouldn't matter to you—you would feel complete freedom. Spiritually speaking, how could you live in a manner that would let the Holy Spirit show you the things of Christ? The fact is that when you are being led by the Spirit you are not under the law. The reason you are not under the law is that you are driving within the speed limit: you are not doing wrong. If you are not doing wrong, there is no law against you. Here is complete freedom.

Some years ago when I was browsing in a bookstore I came across a book whose title, *How to Sleep on a Windy Night,* intrigued me. Set in rural England, the book told how hay is put up in large stacks. Because it rains a great deal the hay is covered with a tarpaulin, which can be ripped away by the wind. How to sleep on a windy night? Put the tarpaulin on in daylight, place stones on the corners, tie it down in such a way that no wind can lift it. Then you can go to bed and sleep on a windy night. There is a profound principle here. Spiritually speaking, walk in the Spirit, be led of the Spirit, and be filled with the Spirit, and you will not be led into the activities of the flesh.

One reason a believer can be so joyful is that he has no fear. The Spirit shows him the things of Christ, and certainty replaces fear. The whole life of a believer is a case of not looking at the evil to avoid it, but looking at the good to do it. The procedure is to think about the Lord, yield to Him, seek His favor, and blessing will follow.

39

The Fruit of the Spirit Is Above the Law

Galatians 5:22-23

Has it ever occurred to you that a Christian need not struggle to achieve virtue?

> But the fruit of the Spirit is love, joy, peace, longsuffering, gentleness, goodness, faith, Meekness, temperance: against such there is no law (Gal. 5:22-23).

There are other translations which reword these descriptions, and sometimes put them in a different order. It will not make much difference which one you prefer. As for me, I don't see any improvement over the King James version. The reading of this description of the conduct of the spiritually minded person is always popular and pleasant. I think that if the whole matter of becoming a believer should be a matter of preferring these nine fruits, there would be 100 percent acceptance. Everybody wants these fruits of the Spirit; and by the way, so far as these fruits are concerned, there would be no big controversy in church over them. No doubt there are differences and controversies in the church but there are no different points of view about the fruit of the Spirit. The difference is in how it is achieved.

Buried in this passage of Scripture there is a still more marvelous idea. In addition to the fact that these are wonderful virtues, there is implicit a profound truth: the believer need not strive for these virtues.

Some people do not claim to be believers and of that I am satisfied they are not particularly proud. I am satisfied some would wish if it were possible to have the blessing that commonly is associated with the believer's experience. I suspect that many do not profess to believe because they would say to themselves: "Very nice if you can get it, but I never could produce it." And they are right; they couldn't produce it. But what they may have missed is that they don't have to: it will be done for them. Such blessing is the fruit of the Spirit, not the goal of the Spirit, or the aim or production of the Spirit. One can understand this if one will consider that apple seeds do not have to strain to produce apples!

We have been bringing to our minds the way the Holy Spirit operates in the heart and mind of the believer. We have noted different statements by Paul, and we have seen how it happens that the Holy Spirit actually moves the believer into doing the will of the Lord Jesus Christ. The word "fruit" is singular: "The fruit of the Spirit is"; then nine specific things are named. The passage does not say "fruits" in the plural. This statement does not say that love is a fruit, joy is a fruit, and so on; the nine traits are not separated. It would appear that all that happens in the believer is the fruit of the Spirit. Because the nine things listed here actually are nine sides of the same thing, they all belong together. This is what is produced in the believer when the Holy Spirit of God is having His way.

There is a certain righteousness of God that comes by faith. Here it is described. You will remember how Scripture said "Walk in the Spirit and you will not fulfil the lust of the flesh." The Holy Spirit manages to move believers to act in this way: unselfishly and not according to their own desires. Believers esteem others better than themselves. How can any human being do this? Only a regenerated person could do these things. This is the fruit of the Spirit: the result of having the Spirit of God moving in the heart.

What does the Holy Spirit do when He shows me the things of Christ? He shows me the grace of the Lord Jesus Christ.

> For ye know the grace of our Lord Jesus Christ, that, though he was rich, yet for your sakes he became poor, that ye through his poverty might be rich (II Cor. 8:9).

The Holy Spirit will show over and over again how the Lord Jesus Christ suffered that sinners might come to know the gospel. "While we were yet sinners, Christ died for the ungodly." Then again the Holy Spirit shows the sufferings of Christ. Every believer should read the story of the crucifixion often. He should read it when he is feeling uncertain about things. It will help him to see how Christ suffered for him. Since God gave His Son to suffer for him, the Holy Spirit can persuade the believer that He will not now allow him to fall away.

Christ Jesus actually yielded Himself to die because He was completely given over to doing the will of His Father. The Holy Spirit will remind the believer of Christ's resurrection. Here the whole mood turns to one of triumph and victory, so that the believer can say about death that "death has lost its sting," and about the grave that "the grave has lost its victory." The things of earth fade away when the things of the Spirit take over. There is no doubt that if the believer will think of the things of Christ, comparing them with his own personal experiences, he will be inclined to loose himself from his own customs and turn himself over to the Lord, trusting in Him, and he will be blessed of the Lord.

40

All Believers Have Access to God by "One Spirit"

Ephesians 2:18

Do you think there will be special favors shown to certain persons before God in heaven?

There is neither Jew nor Greek, there is neither bond nor free, there is neither male nor female: for ye are all one in Christ Jesus (Gal. 3:28).

This brings to mind one of the great truths of the gospel: God is no respecter of persons.

> For through him we both have access by one Spirit unto the Father (Eph. 2:18).

Paul was speaking about the Jews and Gentiles, recognizing that between them, humanly speaking, there were real differences, but rejoicing that in Christ both had equal access to God.

In studying about the Holy Spirit of God, we want to understand more about this arrangement that God has made, that His Holy Spirit should come and be with us. We know that the Bible teaches that God gives the Holy Spirit to all believers. We remember the story of Pentecost, when the Holy Spirit came to dwell in the believers, and we know He has been in the hearts of believers from that time to this present day.

Just what the significance of this is, perhaps, is not always clearly kept in mind. This relationship gives one a certain joy in the Lord, and strength in oneself; there are many blessings if one has the Holy Spirit of God in his heart. We are thinking just now about one thing in particular and that is His effectiveness in bringing together totally different people, such as the Jews and the Gentiles. In general, all people are different: they look different, and they act and think differently; however, their differences do not show up when they stand in the presence of God. People are not compared with each other in the presence of God. Each is a sinner and Christ Jesus died for each man. "All have sinned and come short of the glory of God."

The blessing of God, which is given to those who believe in the Lord Jesus Christ, is a free gift. The sinner does not earn it, he does not qualify for it. He is eligible to receive such blessing not because he is better or worse than someone else. Coming to the Father is in the name of the Lord, not in the sinner's own name. "Whosoever will may come, and whosoever cometh He will in no wise cast out." Since each one comes to God in the name of Christ, in the sight of God his status is equal to that of anyone else.

In history a real difference had developed between Jew and Gentile, and by the time of Jesus of Nazareth there was no social intercourse between them; it was not permitted. For instance, no Gentile was permitted to enter into the temple. A Gentile could be a proselyte and become a Jew, after which he could enter the temple. On the other hand, no Jew was allowed to enter a Gentile home. This was because the possession of the law made the difference: the Jews had the law; the Gentiles did not have the law. This became a barrier, separating the two groups of people. Then came the Christian gospel, and the wonderful truth that the gospel emphasizes before everybody in the whole world: Christ Jesus died for *all* men.

In the first part of Romans, Paul argues that there is no difference between the Jew and the Greek for the reason that all have sinned and come short of the glory of God. Each one is under condemnation, so they are alike in that fashion. Since there is no difference as they stand before God in sin, so there is no difference when they accept Christ; because when they accept Him they stand before God in the Lord Jesus Christ.

Let us look more closely now at the text before us. "For through him [that is, through the Lord Jesus Christ] we both have access by one Spirit unto the Father ['we both' being both Jew and Gentile]." This simply states the profound truth that all men have access by one Spirit—the Holy Spirit—unto the Father. Christ Jesus removes separation between Jews and Gentiles in Himself. In the world? No! In the world all the differences that are between Jews and Gentiles continue to exist. Some years ago while I was thinking about this and trying to understand this truth in my own mind, it came to me something like this: suppose a lady entertained in her home a certain group of people at dinner. Among the friends invited was a lawyer. It was his custom to be attired in a fine broadcloth business suit. But another of her friends was a mechanic. He worked in a garage, and it was his custom to wear coveralls. There would be no way a lawyer dressed in broadcloth could feel comfortable in the presence of a mechanic dressed in denim coveralls, or vice versa. But if these two men joined the Navy and each put on the Navy uniform, they could sit down together and be comfortable. The reason they could be together comfortably would be that the one didn't look like a lawyer and the other didn't look like a mechanic—each looked like a sailor. That's the idea! *In Christ Jesus* there is no difference, and in Him we have access by one Spirit unto the Father.

41

The Spirit Strengthens a Believer to Know the Love of Christ

Ephesians 3:17-18

Do you know what effect would follow if Christ dwelt in the heart of a believer?

For this cause I bow my knees unto the Father of our Lord Jesus Christ, Of whom the whole family in heaven and earth is named, That he would grant you, according to the riches of his glory, to be strengthened with might by his Spirit in the inner man; That Christ may dwell in your hearts by faith; that ye, being rooted and grounded in love, May be able to comprehend with all saints what is the breadth, and length, and depth, and height; And to know the love of Christ, which passeth knowledge, that ye might be filled with all the fulness of God (Eph. 3:14-19).

In this one compact statement Paul covers the whole range or scope of Christian experience. Paul bowed his knees to pray. This should encourage anyone to kneel while praying. Paul's concern was that these believers should be strengthened by the Holy Spirit to receive the presence of Christ in their hearts. It has been previously noted that the Holy Spirit has been given to everyone who is a believer. But the Holy Spirit does not operate to the same extent in every believer's heart. The person who believes in Him and yields to Him has a fuller working of the Spirit within. The Holy Spirit does not arbitrarily force anyone: He will lead. But to the willing-hearted ones He will show the truth of Jesus Christ.

So Paul prays that by the grace of God believers might be strengthened with might by His Spirit in the inner man. "That ye being rooted and grounded in love" is the result of having Christ in the heart. If a person has Christ in his heart he will be conscious of the fact that Christ died for him. "Herein is love, not that we loved God, but that he loved us, and sent his Son to be the propitiation for our sins" (I John 4:10). The fact that Christ Jesus suffered for me is a vivid manifestation of the love of God toward me, and the Holy Spirit will remind me of this. When the Holy Spirit reminds me of this I realize that I am saved because Christ Jesus died for me; in fact I am reconciled to God because Christ died for me. I am actually drawn near to God because Christ patiently prays for me, and all of these things surround me in the love of God.

I am particularly anxious just now that I might speak to those of you who feel personally that you are not strong as believers. If you have the feeling that you really don't amount to much—that you haven't done much—I want you to listen. God will do something for you; God will actually work in you. This is what He will do: He will so affect you by the indwelling of the Holy Spirit of God that the Holy Spirit will enable you to appreciate "what is the breadth, and length, and depth, and height; and to know the love of Christ." He will enable you to appreciate the dimension of the love of God, how great it is: "The love of Christ, which passeth knowledge."

Now, I know that some of you should take time to think about that. How can you know something that passeth knowledge? Have you ever been to the seashore? Have you ever gone to the beach and looked out over the ocean? Just now I am thinking of Santa Monica, California. I am thinking of going out on a fishing boat from that port. When I go out on the boat, I see on the one side the shore line, with the city, traffic, buildings, and everything like that. I look the other way and there is the Pacific Ocean. There is much more to that ocean than I can see. This is what is meant by the passage, "that you might know the love of Christ, which passeth knowledge." This is not for the rare person; this is for you if you are a believer. This is your possible blessing.

So often we treat the believer who speaks of the Lord Jesus personally as if he were queer. If anyone speaks of something the Lord has done for him or something he has done for the Lord, there is the temptation for us to think that person is queer. Actually, that should be the normal. If he should talk to me and never mention the Lord, he would be subnormal as a believer in Christ.

We have noted that the Spirit comes to strengthen the believer so that Christ Jesus might dwell in his heart. Because Christ can be there, and actually dwell there, undoubtedly His presence will produce fruit. Thus that heart can be at peace in communion with God and with others.

But there is something still more wonderful: because Christ is dwelling in the heart the believer can know the love of God. The work of the Holy Spirit which we have emphasized is to take the things of Christ and show them unto us in a way that will affect us. When Christ Jesus is in the heart, that does not make the believer more clever than he was, nor does it take the place of competence or diligence. If a person has Christ Jesus in his heart he will still have to do a day's work. He will still have to act and perform like everybody else. But being rooted and grounded in love, being conscious of the sacrifice of Christ and the meekness and patience of Christ, he may know from experience the love of Christ which passeth knowledge.

In his own heart he may come to appreciate what Christ Jesus has done, that he may be filled will all the fullness of God. In other words, it would mean that he will be totally absorbed in the things of God. This is the marvelous result of having the Holy Spirit working in his heart. I am so glad to think that any one of you who believes in the Lord Jesus Christ may have this. God wants to fill your heart with joy through the Holy Spirit.

42

The Spirit Activates in Believers the Power of God

Ephesians 3:20-21

Have you ever noticed that Christians when praying never doubt that God can? The only concern a Christian ever seems to have when he is praying is whether God will. Any number of times when people come before the Lord in prayer, there is in their hearts a great misgiving that perhaps God does not want to do this thing that they have in mind. It is hardly necessary to emphasize that God could if He wanted to do anything; but there may be some question as to whether He wants to. This question is genuine; this uncertainty on their part has a reason. There is something valid about it because a believer may come before the Lord with his own ideas; he may think he knows and he may feel in his own bones that is his wish and yet not be sure that it is the right thing. So he comes before God and, moved by the Spirit of God, he finds himself actually in the presence of God, ready to say, "nevertheless not my will but thine be done."

Some believers don't go that far; they know all the time that the thing they are saying to God may not be His plan. But seldom do we find anyone who comes into prayer who really has any doubt that God could if He wanted to. When men saw the miracles that Jesus of Nazareth did, they suspected the truth, and asked Him, "Are you the Christ, the Son of God?" They felt that nobody could do the things He had done if He were not God. Nicodemus said that. He was willing to accept Christ Jesus as an authentic teacher because he saw the works that Jesus performed.

I have been much impressed by this attitude of Nicodemus because often among ourselves, people would be inclined to pass judgment on a teacher based on the skill of the teacher's argument. Do you realize that is not what gave Nicodemus his confidence?

What gave Nicodemus his confidence in the Lord Jesus Christ was the effect of His work. "No man can do these things that thou doest except God be with him." Actually the works of God which Christ Jesus performs today are not so much works in the natural world; they are results or works that are achieved in the spiritual world. And these are the evidence of His deity.

There is an amazing statement by Paul that emphasizes the wonderful work of God through Christ. Paul prayed that the Spirit might be in the hearts of the believers and might strengthen them to believe in the indwelling Christ.

> Now unto him that is able to do exceeding abundantly above all that we ask or think, according to the power that worketh in us, Unto him be glory in the church by Christ Jesus throughout all ages, world without end (Eph. 3:20-21).

Just before this Paul drew attention to the fact that if the believer has Christ Jesus operative in his heart, he will know the love of Christ which passes knowledge, and when he knows that he will know something of what God is actually performing in him.

When Scripture says that He "is able to do exceeding abundantly above all that we ask or think," it does not mean that our circumstances will be improved, or that God will give us good health for the next fifty years. This is not what the promise is primarily about. Our Lord did demonstrate His power by applying it in this world—we freely acknowledge that. He opened the eyes of the blind and He made the dumb to talk; He made the deaf to hear and He made the lame to walk. He did all these things in the physical world; and I do not know how many people today are inclined to equate the promises of the Lord Jesus Christ with physical health and happiness and the things of this world. God may very well bless and demonstrate His grace and His power by giving us fortune. But this is not what this context reveals. Conceivably, God may answer prayer to show His power, so that someone may even pray properly for financial help. But Paul is talking about the great work of God that is in Christ Jesus. Christ will make every believer grow as a child of God. This will happen by having Christ in him as the hope of glory.

We cannot imagine how much we can be blessed in God nor what a wonderful fellowship we could have with God the Father. But He will show it to us "according to the power that worketh in us." Elsewhere in Ephesians we are told that the power that worketh in us is the power with which God raised the dead. That is not the power with which He handles the fortunes of war, or the power He has over the crops and the storms at sea. This is the power by which He raises the dead, and by which He transforms us into the likeness of the Lord Jesus Christ. This is the great work of God, that the believer should be born again and be a child of God. This will involve Christ in me, so that I can say afterwards, "Christ liveth in me": so that every man that is in Christ Jesus will be a new creation. The believer by faith is with Christ on the cross, and dies with Christ on the cross; the believer by faith lies with Christ in the grave and is actually disconnected, disoriented, altogether taken out of the things of this world, and is raised from the dead in the newness of life, and now is taken up to be at the right hand of God.

This is the pattern of God's work in Christ Jesus, by which God will accomplish His purpose of creating brethren for His Son. God intends to make all who believe worthy to be a brother, to be one of the brethren among whom the Lord Jesus Christ will be the first. "Unto Him be glory in the church." Now glory in the church occurs when we bear fruit as the children of God. It is because God is working in us to will and to do His good pleasure that there can be glory in the church by Christ Jesus throughout all ages, world without end. Forever, in every way, there will be glory to God in the church by Christ Jesus.

If you have the feeling that this is a deep truth and that this is something that is hard to understand, you are right. But as you read it in Ephesians 3:20-21 and rejoice in it, God is able to do it for you. He can actually make you into something that He can use with the Lord Jesus Christ.

43

The Spirit Provides Unity
in the Body of Christ

Ephesians 4:3

Do you understand how it is that believers from different backgrounds, different families, and different cultures can have unity in their fellowship? "Unity of the Spirit in the bond of peace" (Eph. 4:3). In this way Paul refers to one of the heartfelt interests that every sincere Christian has as he is led by the Holy Spirit: he will want to keep the unity of the Spirit in the bond of peace.

The problem of unity is natural to mankind. From the time that Cain killed Abel, the first two men born into this world as brothers, there has been conflict among men. Now unity—getting together and working together—is essential to corporate life and work. There are various ways of trying to achieve this. Some people try by enforcing a uniformity, making everybody alike so that they will work together. Sometimes the attempt to establish it is by uniting them. John naturally goes his way and Tom naturally goes his way, but John and Tom will try to get together to arrange that both should go the same way. This may prove to be a complicated business but they will try to unite their activities. This is what men mean when they speak of unification. They mean they will take a number of different parts and put them together to make one whole out of them. Whatever method is used, they must unify if anything is to be accomplished. This is the common understanding among men, and the efforts to secure such unity are made in various ways.

An effective and efficient boss has unity. That is because he sees to it everybody does as he wants them to do. It doesn't mean these men work together because they want to; they do it because their job is at stake. Sometimes people seek to secure unity by discussion;

sometimes they will seek to do it by explanation. You can see an obvious example on the football field. In order to accomplish anything eleven men must work together as a unit. A good football team has someone who acts as coach, who manages to influence every man on the squad in such a way that there is a common purpose for all the members of the squad. The plays are worked out in such a way that any time eleven men are on the field they are all going to work together as a group, as a unit. Many of the plays fail because one or another of the men on the team do not carry out their assignments.

There are other examples. Everyone understands that when there is jealousy or ill will, or when there are personalities causing people to differ with each other, the efficiency of that particular group has been ruined.

It is common to think that unity will be achieved if everybody does the same thing. This is notably the case in the army, where efficiency is a matter of life and death. There men operate on the idea that everybody will do one thing, namely, the command that is given. The individual members of the unit are disciplined and trained in such a way that they are to follow no thoughts of their own, beyond doing what they are told to do. Among men generally the purpose to effect unity among independent persons gives rise to something commonly called politics, where one leader tries to get others to work with him in a common cause.

The problem of unity, namely, trying to get people to work together so that they do not conflict with one another, is natural wherever there are men. It is also insoluble. One of the basic characteristics of man is his tendency to develop his own ego: he gets to have his own "I." When an individual grows to being a mature person so that he is considered a well-integrated personality, the "ego" is uppermost. Bringing several egos together becomes a hopeless task.

If anyone should think that well-developed persons could naturally cooperate, he has not watched babies. The baby is a demonstration of human nature as it naturally is. The baby does just exactly what he wants to do, regardless. So far as the baby's attitude toward others is concerned, it is obvious that he couldn't care less about you. Others do not matter to him one bit, nor does any other baby matter to him. He can be interested in people: I can look at him and make faces at him, and he can be interested in that. But if he ever gets anything into his hands, he does not want anybody to take it away from him. If he is in a certain place, he does not want to move somewhere else. One thing a baby can't stand is to be shoved around; he doesn't want anybody doing anything with him different from what he wants done. If one is trying to get people to work together, it is important to start out with them as though they are babies. Naturally each one will be the way he wants to be. Each person grabs for everything and keeps it for himself. If you want people to collaborate, you will have to show them how to work together, to adjust. One person will have to give up, another will have to take over. They will have to negotiate with each other; they will have to select things that they are willing to work out together. If there are five people involved they will want to go in at least five different directions. People are not minded to come together.

Something happened at the Tower of Babel (Genesis 11) that is still operative to this day. Any attempt on anybody's part to secure united action by a group will arouse opposition just as surely as it is tried. It is not strange that in the international world, when people propose some plan for the nations to work together, some exception is immediately taken. That is natural. That is the way it is in the human world. Individual differences with personal interest and ego-sensitivity, jealousy and pride are all aspects of this disposition. Each one goes his own way—that is the way it is. "All we like sheep have gone astray; we have turned every one to his own way . . . " (Isa. 53:6).

In Christ all this is changed, because the Holy Spirit is in each believer. The only thing the believers need to do is to yield to the Spirit that is within them and obey. Remember the illustration of the unity in the Spirit that can be seen in the fingers of your hand.

In the Holy Spirit there is one will. Insofar as the flesh remains in everybody, insofar as everybody stays a human being, he will be in conflict with others. This makes it necessary for believers to endeav-

138

or to keep the unity of the Spirit. The Spirit is unity: He will be one; but I am my own, and I differ from other believers. Tom is his own, Dick is his own, and Harry is his own—each person is his own. When we come together there will be confusion. But if each one of us will yield to the indwelling Holy Spirit of God, the one Spirit will keep us moving together in unity as the fingers of the hand move together. This is one of the blessings of being in Christ Jesus.

44

The Spirit Is "One" in Himself

Ephesians 4:4

Can you think of using the word *one* to refer not to a number but to a relationship?

We are concerned about a believer living the life of faith: living in the Lord. This is an inward experience where we inwardly rest in the Lord and trust in Him; and where we control our various desires because of the indwelling Holy Spirit of God. For instance, I might be tempted to be irritated, but because of the Holy Spirit in me, showing me the patience of Christ, instead of being irritated, I yield myself into His hands and act meekly without irritation.

On another occasion I might in a given situation see things and feel selfish about what I want. I might begin thinking about it and reach for it, but the Holy Spirit in me would show me the mind of the Lord Jesus Christ and would indicate to me how He denied Himself. By showing me these things He would prompt me to yield myself to the will of the Lord Jesus Christ, and this would mean that I would deny myself in that given situation. That would all happen inside me and would be the working of the Holy Spirit.

There are also outward relationships as we live and work with other people. For example, it is a common idea that a group of believers being together as brethren should dwell together in unity: believers are expected to get along with each other. Some people who call themselves believers have strange inclinations. In order to get along with them we will face the problem of reconciling differences. When a person is a true believer in the Lord Jesus Christ, he has in him the Holy Spirit of God. He may not be yielded to the Holy Spirit at all times, and he may not understand the way of the Holy Spirit, but he could learn. He could study the Bible and find out how the Holy Spirit works. If this believer is minded to move in obedience to the indwelling Holy Spirit, which will mean he has denied himself and committed himself to the Lord, then when he comes together with other believers, one idea will prevail in their hearts: their decisions will be in the hands of the Holy Spirit of God. Then there will be unity even though each may act according to his own ability and in his own character; there may be a difference in individual action but in the heart there will be unity. This emphasizes the idea that the believer should have his mind set on being personally willing to yield.

> There is one body, and one Spirit, even as ye are called in one hope of your calling; One Lord, one faith, one baptism, One God and Father of all, who is above all, and through all, and in you all. But unto every one of us is given grace according to the measure of the gift of Christ (Eph. 4:4-7).

Individually believers are different, yet in the heart, with the prevailing Spirit within them, there is a oneness. When we say that there is one Spirit, we do not mean "one" out of "five"; we mean "one" in the sense of "one unit," manipulating many different activities in one will for one purpose. We would say that the human being is integrated in the Lord.

All of this, by the way, is demonstrated in the marriage relationship. The Bible says that when husband and wife come together "they twain shall be one flesh." It does not mean they are one body—with one head, one set of arms and feet. They will be two people with two bodies, but they will be one in their attitudes and in their conduct. This is very important so far as the individual is concerned. In recent years the processes of the mind have received a lot of attention. A word that has become well known is *schizophrenia*—the condition of having a divided mind, and truly there are those who want to go two ways at the same time upon occasion. This is an unfortunate state. We want to give and we want to keep; we want to go and we want to stay. There is a mild aspect of schizophrenia to be seen in us whenever we are torn between two minds on any issue.

Think again of the example of the hand. Hold your hand in front of you and look at the fingers. Each one is different and each moves in a different direction. Shut your hand and the five fingers will collaborate. There is one fist if you will; there is one hand exercised in a handshake; one hand that handles scissors and needle; one hand that writes with the pen. Yet there are five fingers operating in a unity that does not come from training. This is because of the one mind that controls them. Now, all of this brings to mind the general function of the Spirit to direct the church. As each one in the church does as he is led by the Holy Spirit there will be harmony; this will result in power. Led by the Spirit there will be no contention, no conflict, and really no division. To be led by the Spirit involves self-denial but it brings great blessing.

45

The Spirit Can Be Grieved

Ephesians 4:29-30

Have you any idea what it would take to grieve the Holy Spirit?

> Let no corrupt communication proceed out of your mouth, but that which is good to the use of edifying, that it may minister grace unto the hearers. And grieve not the holy Spirit of God, whereby ye are sealed unto the day of redemption (Eph. 4:29-30).

Of course, we understand very well nobody living is good enough to live perfectly as a member of the body of Christ. Being good in yourself is not the way you get to be a true believer. Any person may become a believer by accepting and receiving Jesus Christ as his Savior and Lord. He needs only to open his heart and receive the Holy Spirit of God; thus he can receive the grace of God in Christ Jesus. He only needs to yield himself to Christ.

In this study of the Holy Spirit we are addressing our comments to believers. The Holy Spirit is God Himself in the heart of any believer, operative there, doing the will of God. The Holy Spirit is a person; He is one of the three persons in the Godhead. As such a person, He dwells in our hearts. He is with us at all times.

"Corrupt communication" in verse 29 is a form of speech you and I might not ordinarily use. A communication that is corrupt is something that would destroy or defile. Believers should not say anything that will hurt another or that is irreverent so far as God is concerned. The language itself as translated here should probably be translated like this, "corrupting communication," viz., don't say anything that spoils anybody. Talk that is careless can be corrupting. There are ways of saying things that are suggestive; some people say things about the Bible in such a way that if you followed their suggestions you would not believe the Bible. This admonition from Ephesians 4:29 comes in a section of this letter where Paul outlines how to promote Christian character. He actually shows how to build a Christian personality; in other words, he describes how a Christian can train himself so that his manner of life will be consistent with his profession of faith in the Lord Jesus Christ. For example, "Put on the new man, which after God is created in righteousness and true holiness" (verse 24); then in verse 25, "putting away lying, speak every man truth with his neighbor." This is a very simple way of putting it. It is easy to understand what that means: do you want to stop lying? Tell the truth. That is all it will take.

Again Paul says, "Let no corrupt communication proceed out of your mouth, but that which is good to the use of edifying, that it may minister grace to the hearers" (verse 29). In other words, if I have a story to tell that is a bit shady, I should not tell it; I should tell only that which is good and clean. The Holy Spirit will be grieved if my tongue appeals to personal interest, if I talk about things that arouse people to think selfishly or wrongfully. And if I teach in Sunday school and do not refer to the Bible, if I just try to build up in my pupils what can come from the goodness of human nature, this will not please the Lord or the Holy Spirit. We should always keep in mind that Christians will be guided if they remember one principle: when they talk, they should try to talk in such a way that the Holy Spirit will not be grieved. In that case what they say will be good.

46

The Holy Spirit Produces Fruit Worthy of "Children of Light"

Ephesians 5:9

What kind of conduct would you expect of a person who claimed to be led by the Holy Spirit? If we take the Bible to be true, we can feel confident that it is a revelation from God to help us and guide us. Salvation is of God. Our confidence is that God will do it, but it seems that many people do not know how this operates.

Persons who have accepted Jesus Christ as Savior can be considered as being spiritually minded, and those who have not yet accepted Christ will be considered as natural people. In presenting the gospel to the world we would like to show the natural man how things really work. We want him to know what Christ Jesus would do for anybody who believes in Him. It is like having a class in which a lecturer talks about married life to both married and single people. Those who are married are actually in the process of having a home, but those not yet married could listen and profit. Some of you already walk with the Lord Jesus Christ; you may not be doing much and you may stumble quite a bit, but you do believe in Him and you are counting on Him to save your soul. Then there are those of you who for one reason or another have not committed yourselves to live in the way of the Lord Jesus Christ—you have not taken Him as your Savior. You may not yet be the kind of person I refer to when I talk about a Christian but you might be interested and you could become one.

In Ephesians 5:9 we read, "For the fruit of the Spirit is in all goodness and righteousness and truth." What this points out is what will happen in anybody who comes to Jesus Christ as Savior, yields himself to Jesus Christ, is willing to let the Holy Spirit take over his thinking and bring about the things of the will of God. For such a person certain results will follow. The Spirit will guide him in his conduct. Paul summarized this when he said the results which he calls the fruit will be in all goodness and righteousness and truth.

Whenever one thinks about the Christian gospel and the Christian experience, he should always start out with God, the Creator of the heavens and the earth. God is always the same: holy, just, righteous, and pure; and God is of such a nature that He requires righteousness among His people. There are some human beings God will save forever. He will regenerate them, give them eternal life, and keep them with His Son, Jesus Christ. God requires of His people that they produce righteousness. God satisfies every need of His people, and so they do the things that He requires.

It is man's duty to be as God wants him to be. He may try to do this according to the law of Moses, but the truth is that man is unable in himself to do that which is right. The reason for that is that he is sinful. Because of sin man is selfish, so he wants to be serving himself. This is the reason that when a man wants to begin the Christian life, he must begin by turning to the Lord Jesus Christ. When a person turns to God the first thing involved is the denial of self: the crucifying of the flesh. Then he can be raised from the dead to live in the newness of life. This is the situation so far as any man is concerned. No natural man does the will of God—he must be born again. The wonderful fact is that any man can accept Christ. When once He has been accepted, it is Christ in a person that will produce goodness, righteousness, and truth.

The Holy Spirit takes the things of the Lord Jesus Christ and shows them unto me, inclining my heart to trust in the Lord. The Holy Spirit will so affect, causing me to yield myself to the mind of God, and thereby produce goodness and righteousness and truth. Thus the Spirit produces fruit worthy of the children of light.

We need to recognize that human beings can try to produce goodness; they can try to be honest; but only the Holy Spirit of God can produce these virtues in and through His operation within the individual soul.

47

It Is Imperative that a Believer Should "Be Getting Filled with the Spirit"

Ephesians 5:18

Do you think you understand about being filled with the Spirit? Everyone who has ever heard the Christian gospel will have heard of the Holy Spirit. Anybody who knows what the Bible teaches will know that the New Testament speaks about the Holy Spirit being given to believers; and about certain believers being filled with the Spirit. Some may wonder what that means; and it is somewhat hard to grasp because the Spirit is not anything corporeal. The Spirit is invisible. If the Spirit is invisible, how would one know if he were filled? The idea of being filled with the Spirit is also difficult to understand.

If one were to say that a certain room was filled with light, would that make sense? If there were dark places in the room it could not be said that the room was filled with light; however, if it was daylight, the daylight would fill the entire room, even the dark corners. There actually would not be any dark corners because light would shine everywhere. Or one could say that a certain schoolhouse was filled with noise. What would that mean? It would mean no one could go anywhere in the schoolhouse where he would be without noise.

Many who come to God want to come piecemeal, so to speak. It seems at times that some come to God about the way they go to church: once a week. There are probably any number of people who, if they live through each day of the week and then go to church on Sunday for an hour, feel they have worshiped God. God was present everywhere all week and there is no particular reason why one should think that because he goes to church on Sunday morning, he has worshiped God for the week.

In my heart I may actually acknowledge the reality of God and I may think in terms of having a relationship with God; and still I may not have my mind filled with God. There will be times, when I am in church and the preacher is preaching from the very Word of God, that I will be thinking about a football game or going fishing. In such cases my mind is certainly not filled with the thoughts of God; I am thinking of things of my own doing. Just as one day a week isn't all the time, so one hour a day isn't all the time. One could say that about turning to God, because I think of Him, I read the Bible, I think of Him when I drive my car or when I kneel in prayer with someone. This may all be good! But in between such times there is much time when I don't think of Him. If I were in such a frame of mind that every conscious thought I had, everything that went through my mind related to the reality of the Holy Spirit, then it would be true to say that I was filled with the Holy Spirit.

Paul lays down a very definite imperative in Ephesians 5:18: "And be not drunk with wine, wherein is excess; but be filled with the Spirit." Isn't it amazing to find those two ideas in one sentence? In what sense would they be alike? Actually each one stimulates one aspect of the human personality: wine stimulates the flesh; the Holy Spirit stimulates the spirit of man.

In order for anyone to be filled with the Spirit, he must pay attention to spiritual things. If you are going to be drunk with wine you have to drink it. Don't think that is as simple as it sounds. A person could have a lot of wine in the cellar but if he did not take any of it into his mouth he would never be drunk. He has to take it in and let it affect him. But he must be careful not to let it affect him too much, "wherein is excess." The same is true with the Spirit: "But be filled with the Spirit." There are some things that anybody would have to do to be filled with the Spirit. Basically, of course, he must accept Jesus Christ; that means an individual has to deny himself. Anyone could be stopped right there. If he will not deny himself, take up his cross and follow Christ, everything else is out. The second thing is that God will regenerate him. He need not work at it: God will do that. After that God will send His Holy Spirit into his heart. He will not have to work on that, either. God will do it. Then he must receive the Holy Spirit; he must recognize the Holy Spirit as being given to him from God, and he must yield to the indwelling Holy Spirit. As the sunlight fills a room when the shade is drawn, so He will fill you. Notice that the careful translation is "be ye getting filled with the Spirit." This is referred to grammatically as the continuous imperative. In other words, a person is not filled once for all. Just because at one time he was experiencing the fullness of God does not mean he will have it for all time; but he can be filled again and again, if he will maintain his yielded obedience to Him. If he will walk with Him, He will fill him for sure.

48

The Sword of the Holy Spirit
Is the Word of God

Ephesians 6:17

Did you know that the Bible claims to be the very language the Holy Spirit will use when He communicates the mind of God to man?

And take the helmet of salvation, and the sword of the Spirit, which is the word of God (Eph. 6:17).

Paul is here describing the preparation of a believer for the battle that he must wage against the evil in the spiritual world. "Put on the whole armour of God, that ye may be able to stand against the wiles of the devil" (Eph. 6:11). Paul describes this armor and the various parts with their spiritual significance. The word "sword," of course, is a figure of armament, and Paul indicates when he calls the Word of God the sword of the Spirit that the Bible is the tool the Holy Spirit uses in accomplishing spiritual ends.

In our day it is a very common thing to say that God can and will use other means than Scripture to communicate His will. In fact that is heard so often it is easy to assume everybody thinks so and everybody knows it: but this is not what the Bible reveals. The Bible does not indicate any other way. Someone may say, "Do you mean to say that God will use only the words of Scripture?" And to that I would say, "Yes." If that person were to say, "I don't see how you can say that," I wouldn't be a bit surprised: any number of people don't see it. The one thing I have learned is not to be surprised at unbelief; you find it everywhere. The reason I would answer as I have indicated is this very fact: Scripture is the means used by the Holy Spirit to communicate the truth of Jesus Christ.

Some years ago when I was present as a speaker at a Bible conference, after the evening address I was participating in a forum meeting. I was asked point blank whether I was saying that the canon of Scripture that we commonly call the Holy Bible is all there is to reveal about Jesus Christ. I said, "Yes, that is what I was claiming." I could feel the shock of this simple statement on that company. They thought that my answer showed I was very limited. Why would I think that God would stop all revelation over 1900 years ago? I let them talk. After awhile I asked, "What argument can you put up, that there should be continuing revelation?" I then pointed out that the Bible says "In the beginning was the Word, and the Word was with God, and the Word was God. The same was in the beginning with God" (John 1:1-2). Then Scripture goes on to say, "And the Word was made flesh, and dwelt among us, and we beheld His glory" (John 1:14). The Word was made flesh when Jesus of Nazareth became incarnate.

In continuing the discussion I pointed out, "When the Lord Jesus came into this world and lived as Jesus of Nazareth, there was only one Jesus of Nazareth. He lived and He died. When He said on the cross, 'It is finished,' I think He put a period to indicate the end of His revelation. That was the end. It was finished." Some of those present asked, "Don't you think God could add more?" I answered, "If He will bring Jesus Christ back into this world and have Him live a little longer, and let Him do a little more and use that, then I'll say there is more. But I will also say that Jesus of Nazareth was the perfect Word of God. 'He that hath seen me hath seen the Father.' "

The very fact that God saw fit to reveal Himself in this world and make Himself incarnate in one person, who lived one life that ended in death at Calvary, indicates that is everything: there is no more. Many things have happened that are not written in the Bible. The people and the nations and all the business that goes on in the world are not described in the Bible. That is true! But what is described in the Bible is God's plan of salvation, and that is described completely. The whole revelation is there before you because it was all in Jesus Christ, who lived once, died once, and was raised from the grave and taken at once into heaven in the ascension; He is there now.

That is the answer I gave on that occasion. Another way I could have answered would have been with reference to the work of Jesus of Nazareth. We remember His temptation in the desert, and that the words He used in answering Satan were all words of Scripture. Many times when He would reason with people about natural processes He would turn to nature. When He reasoned about the logic of a thing He would appeal to their rational understanding, but when He undertook to show them something that was revealed He would say, "How readest thou?" and He would call their attention to Scripture.

Our Lord Jesus said with reference to Scripture that not one jot nor one tittle would pass from the law till all was fulfilled. When the Lord Jesus was on Calvary's cross, dying and praying to His Father, He quoted from the 22nd Psalm, "My God, My God, why hast Thou forsaken me?" After His resurrection, when He was raised from the dead, if anyone could have talked about the resurrection from personal experience, it would have been Jesus of Nazareth. But what He did is a matter of record: He opened their understanding that they might understand Scripture. If there were any other way of revelation of the gospel you might expect to find believers somewhere that the Bible has not gone. But this is not true. In all of history in all the world, where the Bible has not been there are no believers. The Bible is the instrument—the sword of the Spirit.

Something that for the present has caught the fancy of some is "wordless communication." It is true that sometimes the lifting of an eyebrow or a shrug of the shoulders conveys a lot. But if you ever want to hear what people really mean and you ask them again, "What did you say?" that is the thing that counts. God uses the Word, the sword of the Spirit. The Word spoken by the prophets and the apostles, the Word written as we have it in Scripture, and the Word incarnate in Jesus of Nazareth: these are God's means of revealing to man His marvelous grace in Jesus Christ—that He will save those who come unto God by Him.

49

The Holy Spirit Enables the Believer to Pray with Perseverance

Ephesians 6:18-20

Would you have any idea what it would take to keep a man praying with confidence when the answer is being delayed?

Praying always with all prayer and supplication in the Spirit, and watching thereunto with all perseverance and supplication for all saints; And for me, that utterance may be given unto me, that I may open my mouth boldly, to make known the mystery of the gospel, For which I am an ambassador in bonds: that therein I may speak boldly, as I ought to speak (Eph. 6:18-20).

This is the way the apostle Paul encouraged the believers at Ephesus to pray. I am interested in bringing to your attention how he urged them to pray always with all prayer and supplication in the Spirit.

For many of us praying is often a matter of impulse. I know that some who pray do not count themselves as believers. They may be in favor of the gospel as a whole, in favor of church work and things that pertain to the Lord Jesus Christ, but they personally are not having personal dealings with Him. The one thing such persons need to do is to come to the Lord Jesus Christ. For those of us who have come and who are trusting in Christ Jesus, we are going on living in this world; but our trust is in "nothing less than Jesus' blood and righteousness." For those I want to say something about praying. Often when we feel like it, we pray; unless we feel like it, we don't pray. Sometimes we have to feel very much like it before we pray at all. That depends on the individual person and his experience. We may think of some big thing that we want, so we pray for it. We pray big requests. Then there may be times when we have been praying for something perhaps a couple of days or a week or so, and on impulse we quit. Asked why, we couldn't even tell you. We just say, "Well, I thought it was a good idea." Actually we didn't have a good reason to quit asking God to help.

There are other times when we are actually filled with dismay and with fear because all of our activity, all of our participation in prayer was largely a matter of personal feelings and of personal contact with other people. This is what we are thinking about just now. Whenever we pray under these circumstances we will find that we are not always moved to pray, and when we do pray we are inclined to do so because we think it is the thing to do or we are hoping to get something by it, whatever it is, or whatever the occasion may be.

It is a very common thing for us to be very earnest and fervent in prayer for a length of time, and then shortly thereafter to stop praying altogether. It seems that the winds blow hot, and then they blow cold. Sometimes we do and sometimes we don't. James has something to say about that:

> But let him ask in faith, nothing wavering. For he that wavereth is like a wave of the sea driven with the wind and tossed. For let not that man think that he shall receive any thing of the Lord (James 1:6-7).

It is true that we will receive things if we ask from God, and especially if we ask in faith; but when James said "let him ask in faith" he meant not only that at the moment you asked you believed, but that generally you believe in God. You believe in God and because you believe, you pray. When you ask in faith your whole outlook is one of faith. You have faith about the creation, about the providence of God, and you have faith about everything that has to do with the very life which you are living.

This may be the way it is with any believer who has confidence in God. Such a person will pray according to the way James says it: "But let him ask in faith, nothing wavering." This person will not pray in fits and starts: "now you do and now you don't"; strong one time, weak the next. Not like that! The person who wavers is "like a wave of the sea driven by the wind and tossed." We could ask ourselves how could we overcome that. How will we become steady in our faith and steadfast in our praying? This is the function of the Holy Spirit of God. When the Spirit is operative in a person He keeps the things of Christ before his eyes vividly. You might ask, "What things?" For example, the death of Christ. "He that spared not his own Son, but delivered him up for us all, how shall he not with him also freely give us all things?" (Rom. 8:32). Thinking of how the Spirit keeps the things of Christ before the eyes of a believer, we are reminded that "God commendeth his love toward us, in that, while we were yet sinners, Christ died for us" (Rom. 5:8).

The Holy Spirit will keep the way of Christ before us. He does not have to bring Christ Jesus to death again. He doesn't have to induce the Lord to come down from heaven at each generation; He came once and for all. The Holy Spirit will make the believer feel that the whole truth of Christ Jesus is for him. Consider another passage about the Lord:

> Wherefore he is able also to save them to the uttermost that come unto God by him, seeing he ever liveth to make intercession for them (Heb. 7:25).

To be reminded of this is the work of the Holy Spirit. The whole idea that Christ Jesus is able to save will be brought to mind and kept in the mind. "And [He shall] bring all things to your remembrance, whatsoever I have said unto you" (John 14:26). This again is the work of the Holy Spirit of God. The fact that Christ Jesus has died will not change; that Christ Jesus has already been raised from the dead is a fact that will not change, and that Christ Jesus did go up into the presence of God will not change. That He is coming again in the will of God is forever true.

When the individual sees these things, he can be brought close to the Lord and reconciled to God; this again is the kind of thing the Holy Spirit does. He strengthens the believer to continue in the things that are pleasing to God in Christ Jesus, so that he can follow through and be praying always with all prayer and supplication in the Spirit. The Holy Spirit will remind the believer of the reality and the power of God, and of His way of doing things. As he is reminded of these things, he will be able to believe the grace and the mercy of God.

This, then, is the way it works. The Holy Spirit shows the way of the Lord Jesus Christ unto the believer, and thus actually reminds him of what Christ Jesus did once and for all. The Holy Spirit, therefore, will always be the doer, and believers will always receive from Him.

50

The Holy Spirit Strengthens the Believer Facing Persecution

Philippians 1:19

Do you know what strengthens a believer to face persecution?

For I know that this shall turn to my salvation through your prayer, and the supply of the Spirit of Jesus Christ (Phil. 1:19).

These are words that the apostle Paul wrote to the church at Philippi, and they show the confidence he feels as he goes on to face the persecution that is ahead. He might even meet death, but he is confident that he will be strengthened for it, and that he would be kept strong by the working of the Holy Spirit within his heart.

All around us, here and there, is evidence of what God has done for us. For instance, when we are facing any given situation where there is trouble, the Holy Spirit will remind us that God gave His own Son for us. We will have such thoughts as this: if God gave His own Son to die for us, will He not also with Him freely give us all things? It isn't a question of God one day in the future doing something on our behalf; He has already given the Lord Jesus Christ for us, and this is a very strengthening thought. God has also given us His Holy Spirit; we know this is true because the Bible says so, and there has been evidence that God Himself is with us. We are conscious of the fact that God gave His Holy Spirit for this very purpose, that the Spirit would remember the things of God and strengthen us to endure whatever comes to pass. This truth becomes operative in us and we are made strong in faith, giving glory to God.

We also have the Bible. The Bible has in it many precious promises, and we can take courage. God gave us those precious promises; He gave to us the Holy Spirit and sent His only begotten Son and had Him die for us. Inasmuch as God has done all these things, it is not hard for us to be strengthened today in the confidence that God will not now forsake us. He actually has in mind to bring us through to Himself.

Suppose that today I come into a situation that is hard for me to bear. Perhaps I am being misunderstood or criticized unjustly. Maybe I am being in some way left to myself or put under an extra load, and no one seems to care. God will remind me in my darkest hour that in days gone by the Holy Spirit Himself came to bring me strength and comfort. I can remember what God has done in the past and I am encouraged to believe He will do it again tomorrow. The Holy Spirit will bring these things to my mind and strengthen me so that I can be steadfast in my confidence.

Then again, the Holy Spirit will remind me of the providence of God. I have home, friends, loved ones, and I have opportunity. I have health and strength, and any number of things in providence that were arranged and provided for me. I am reminded of all this. And so it is with reference to God's mercy. There are times that I can remember some situation when I would have understood very well if God had let everything drop in on me. It would have been easy for me to understand if God had allowed my life to be snuffed out in certain situations. But He didn't. He gave me His mercy and kindness, His gentleness and His goodness. The Holy Spirit will remind me of these things, and I will be encouraged. The Holy Spirit also reminds me of what God has done for others, because there have been other people who have had problems, and He helped them to endure those things.

Even though I have not seen the Lord in person, and even though there is no way for me to claim that I have had any manifestation from God that I could recognize, at the same time the Holy Spirit will show me the things of Christ. It is good for me to take time to recall what God has already done. I can remember that famous verse in the Old Testament, "Hitherto hath the Lord helped us." Maybe I have had a vivid experience of conversion, or I passed through a time of great sorrow when I felt as though I would break, and then at that time I remembered the Lord Jesus Christ, so that I was able to go through with things that I never would have believed I could. God gave me grace and God gave me strength.

So I can say with Paul, "I know that this shall turn to my salvation through your prayer, and the supply of the Spirit of Jesus Christ," and this will strengthen me so that I can continue to bear witness to the Lord Jesus Christ regardless of what lies ahead. This the Holy Spirit of God does for each of us.

51

The Holy Spirit Makes Fellowship Among Believers Actual

Philippians 2:1

Do you realize what makes fellowship among Christians so strong?

> If there be therefore any consolation in Christ, if any comfort of love, if any fellowship of the Spirit, if any bowels and mercies, Fulfil ye my joy, that ye be likeminded, having the same love, being of one accord, of one mind (Phil. 2:1-2).

The apostle Paul wrote this to the church members at Philippi, urging them to be united and to strengthen each other. He wanted them to know the fellowship of the Holy Spirit, "having the same love, being of one accord, of one mind."

A number of self-evident conditions are mentioned in this verse. For instance, we know there is such a thing as being comforted in

Christ Jesus; this being the case, we should then with all believers be able to walk in the ways of God. What a wonderful thing it is to have other believers with you, to be one of a company of people who care for one another! It is natural for us to think in terms of ourselves, and when we know a group of people who are affected by the Holy Spirit of God we find that they are interested in and they love one another. When Paul uses the phrase, "if any bowels and mercies," this is a reflection of the psychology of the day when it was believed that in the sympathetic nervous system your feelings were grounded in the organs of your viscera. If you are highly elated about anything you feel good all over, but if you are depressed you don't feel good inside; actually, if you are in great distress you could have indigestion.

Nothing in the world is so good for everyday health and strength as good will among the brethren, being with people who don't quarrel. You can rest and relax when you are with those who are not contentious.

This is what Paul means when he says that "if there be any such thing as a consolation in Christ," if you can get any comfort out of being a believer; if you are inwardly strengthened and encouraged at all; or if you have any emotions of kindness and graciousness to each other at all, "fulfil ye my joy, that ye be likeminded, having the same love, being of one accord, of one mind." This is the fellowship of the Holy Spirit. Among people who believe there are what can be called reconciled hearts. Such a heart is turned over to the Lord. Once the person walked away from Him; now he walks with Him. Once he disobeyed Him; now he wants to do His will. Once it was hard for him to read the Bible; now he reads it joyfully because he wants to find out more about it. There has been a change—he has been reconciled to God. If that is true with any one believer, it is also true with others. When they get together there is a new joy in their personal spiritual fellowship as they are together in the Lord. Those who are believers in the Lord Jesus Christ walk with Him and don't ever want to leave Him. There are others like that, so he will be one with other brethren, each of whom is regenerated by the grace of God. Such persons will be very close to each other, because the Holy Spirit works in them. This is what Paul has in mind in this passage—since there is such a thing as the fellowship of the Spirit, then believers should fulfill the joy of Paul, that they be likeminded, having the same love, being of one accord and of one mind.

The things that are in Scripture have been given to all men who believe. The indwelling of the Holy Spirit in the heart makes a person feel that everyone else who is also a believer belongs. This gives a fellowship and a unity. The Holy Spirit releases this unity by the grace of God. Unregenerate human beings are not of one mind. If you bring two natural people together you have two ideas. If you bring four people together you have four ideas. That is the way it is with human beings—each goes his own way. But when you become a believer you will find fellowship with others who also believe in the Lord Jesus Christ, and in whose hearts the Holy Spirit dwells. This fellowship will be sweet because it will strengthen you, even as you will strengthen the other. A twofold cord is not easily broken. All of this is made possible because the Holy Spirit works in every believer, showing the things of Christ. As He does this in me, I am made to realize that I am related to other believers and other believers are related to me.

52

The Spirit Operates in the Believer to Activate the Will of God

Philippians 2:13

Do you know what prompts a believer to obey the will of God? I realize very well that there are those who believe Jesus is Christ but who have never ever done anything about receiving the Holy Spirit into their hearts. But such persons need to recognize that if they are true believers, if they believe in the Lord Jesus Christ and are trusting Him for the salvation of the soul, then God has already put His Holy Spirit into their hearts. At the same time I'll have to say that if anyone does not believe what Scripture reveals about this, if he does not yield himself to the indwelling Holy Spirit of God, then the things of Christ will not take root. Such a person would possibly claim that he has been saved by the grace of God in Christ Jesus and that God has shown him that he belongs to Him, but if he were asked whether or not he has received the Holy Spirit he might be vague and might even turn away, unless he had come to know the indwelling Spirit of God.

It is important to know that the believer can be helped to obey the will of God by a prompting from within that is the result of the indwelling Holy Spirit. I realize there are those who have not had this experience, and because of that such persons might have some difficulty in following me just now. I will be talking about something that such a person has not yet experienced. It is a blessed truth that God is no respecter of persons, that whosoever will may come unto Him, and whosoever cometh unto Him, He will in no wise cast out. The fact is God has given His Holy Spirit that people should be blessed, that human beings should have this great privilege if they will. But He works only in those who yield themselves to God. Paul referred to this when he wrote "For it is God which worketh in you both to will and to do of his good pleasure" (Phil. 2:13).

How does the Holy Spirit work in you? What does the Holy Spirit do? The Holy Spirit reminds me of the price that was paid for me by Christ Jesus; He will also remind me that I am not my own. Suppose, for instance, that I, as a believer, should prefer to live alone. When I am thinking about this and am tempted to be that way, the Holy Spirit will remind me that I am not alone, that I have within me the very presence of God, and because of this I am going to want to be brotherly toward other believers.

The Holy Spirit also will remind me that I have been crucified with Christ. If, in the course of living, it dawns on me that I am not being favored, and that there are certain things I have been doing that people belittle, I could be tempted to be hurt. But the Holy Spirit will remind me that I have been crucified with Christ; I should reckon myself to be "dead indeed unto sin." If I will actually put this into effect and reckon myself dead, I could be surprised how the feeling of insult, the feeling of hurt, will fade out of my memory.

The Holy Spirit will also deliver me from this present evil world. So far as I am concerned: when I go out in the world, I am no match for it. The things of the world are too close to me—they appeal to me. It is very hard for me to deny my interest in the things round about me when I am conscious of them, because that is just like denying myself. This is the kind of thing the Holy Spirit overcomes. This is a new and different thing; and it is something that God works out for His people. God actually uses His people to bring His will to pass. I would not have to be anybody special for that; I do not have to be a missionary or a minister or a Bible class teacher. All I need to be is a poor sinner before God, someone just trusting, who would be ready to say from my heart "God be merciful to me a sinner."

The Holy Spirit, reminding me that Christ Jesus died for me, is also inclined to remind me that Almighty God is the Father of all those who put their trust in the Lord Jesus Christ. And since I did receive the Lord Jesus Christ, and I did put my trust in Him and am resting upon Him, in that way I come before God. The grace of God, released from within, affects all aspects of living; His grace makes me conscious of the fact that I belong to Him. The Holy Spirit will show me that the glory of God is involved. It is important for God to bless me because if God will help me and bless me, His name will be glorified. The Holy Spirit shows me that for the will of God to be done I will have to do my part and if I respond God will work out His will. So the Word of God is brought to mind and because I am a believer in the Lord Jesus Christ and because He used the Word of God, I will use the Word of God; and the same Holy Spirit who moved the men who wrote it now moves in the hearts of those who listen, that they might believe.

The Holy Spirit does not speak of Himself; He shows me the things of Christ and reminds me of these things that have been done for me. In this way the Holy Spirit of God actually enables me to serve the Lord and to live and walk with Him, because He watches over me and keeps me, leading me along the way by His grace and mercy. I am to give Him the praise and the glory, and I am to trust that God will continue to glorify Himself through me and to all other people.

53

The Holy Spirit Operates by Enabling Believers to Realize "Christ in You"

Philippians 4:13

Have you any idea how it is that a believer can deny himself and suffer loss without distress?

> I can do all things through Christ which strengtheneth me (Phil. 4:13).

When believers say that they can do all things it is well to think carefully of the meaning. There are many things a believer does that are just natural to him for which he does not need the help of the Holy Spirit, e.g., the ordinary activities of making a living, etc. So far as a believer is concerned, people may overlook the fact that he believes in Christ because he is a good teacher or a good mechanic. So far as he is concerned, he will be able to live his life in an ordinary, natural way. The believer needs only to be confident and to be diligent in his daily affairs and he will be able to adorn the gospel because he is a good man. There is no direct way in which we can say that Christ will strengthen him to sweep the floor or help him to drive a car.

It is true that the presence of the Lord will be a blessing to me. I recognize that; but so far as my activities as a human being are concerned, they are as they are because I am human. For instance, if I have unfriendly, unkind neighbors I should be patient and long-suffering with them. In a case like that I need help; as I need help to be meek when someone does me an injustice. These are the things we are concerned with when we say "I can do all things through Christ which strengtheneth me." In all matters where my judgment is involved about things I should do, when I am counting on God to do them in me and through me by the work of the Holy Spirit of God, in all such cases I am to keep in mind that God will do these things. He will bring things to pass so that I can do all things along the line of being longsuffering, meek and humble, and kind. In matters where it is the will of God that I must deny myself and where my best intentions would fail, by His Spirit He will help me to do them. Looking at that verse and considering it will reveal that this result depends upon the operation of the Holy Spirit. I have used the term *His Spirit* as over against Christ Jesus, when I spoke of Christ Jesus as using His Spirit, but you understand how closely these things work together. For instance, when people talk as though God were in a cathedral, and when we think about worshiping God and

163

planning to go to church to do it, I know quite well that God is in me, as He is in every believer. I am always ready to *say* on occasion that He is in me and in every believer.

Many talk about God as if He were in a church, but I know that He is in people. When the opportunity comes this is something I should speak out about. I will have the courage to do this because the Holy Spirit has already committed Himself to enable me to live and to act that way. When others are talking lightly about spiritual things (speaking of how men were brought to heaven or allowed to go to hell), the thing for me, of course, is *not* to do it. At the same time there is another thing I may have to do if I am living in the Lord and trusting in His Holy Spirit: suppose a good many of my friends in the church were planning a fishing trip on Sunday. What should I do? I don't have to condemn them, but I must separate myself. I am no longer able to lead those people: they separated from me. So that if everyone else is planning a fishing trip on Sunday and I don't want to go, if I feel deep down in my heart that God would not want me to go, the Holy Spirit will work in my heart to enable me to refuse. How will He do this? He will show me the things of Christ.

When people around me are not obeying the law and are not honest with their income tax, how can I as a Christian give a good testimony for the Lord Jesus Christ? How can I differ from them and be humbly respectful to them and obedient to God? The Holy Spirit enables me to do this. When I feel that I need all of the money I have, and a plea comes from missions, what enables me to give to missions? The indwelling Holy Spirit of God will enable me to do the right thing. Again, when no one else seems to want to pray—when actually people praying are just saying words, and when I have the feeling that they are saying the words just to be finished with them, how could I personally be fervent in prayer? Here, too, I can do all things through Christ which strengtheneth me.

Christ will be in me because of the Holy Spirit. He takes the things of Christ and shows them unto me, so that as I am a believing person, as I live my life, I will find myself being kept aware of Calvary, where Christ died for me; of the grave where Christ was buried for me; of the resurrection, when Christ rose from the dead to the glory of God; of the ascension, when He went to heaven on behalf of all who believe. The descent into hell is something that is recorded as plain as day, just as are all these things that we are thinking about just now. The Holy Spirit keeps me aware of these things, keeps me affected by them; and because He does, I can do all things that are in the will of God, through Christ which strengtheneth me. The Holy Spirit is strengthening me in the inner man that Christ Jesus may dwell in my heart by faith.

54

The Spirit Promotes Love in the Brethren

Colossians 1:8

Do you think Christians love each other only because they are nice people? Much attention is given in these days to the doctrine of the Holy Spirit; if one talks about the Spirit at all, he usually speaks of what should be taught about Him, or of the receiving of the Holy Spirit, so that the conditions under which He could be received are discussed.

Our interest in these studies is in what actually happens in the heart. Granted that the Holy Spirit is real, and that He is the third person of the Godhead, that He has come to be with the believers, who have received Him because God has put Him there, what happens in the heart of a believer under these circumstances? The apostle Paul wrote this about Epaphras, "Who also declared unto us your love in the Spirit" (Col. 1:8). Here Paul recognized the fact that these Colossian believers were really interested in him and had an attitude of affection toward him; and he also knew where that attitude on their part came from. It was because of the indwelling Holy Spirit, and Epaphras had recognized it. When he described how the believers in Colossae acted, he took note of the fact that their actions were grounded in the work of the Holy Spirit: "your love in the Spirit."

In the New Testament love is not so much a matter of sentiment or feeling as it is a description of conduct. If one does things in such a way that respect is shown to those in authority, and consideration is shown to those people around him, if he acts in charity toward those who are unfortunate, he has been acting in love. This action in the believer had its origin in the Holy Spirit. When the believer loves anyone it is not because that person is worthy. He may be worthy or he may be unworthy; the believer will love him anyway. This does not necessarily mean that the believer approves of that person, or that he likes him; but the believer can love him because love is not grounded in that person, nor in that family the believer may be helping. And it is not necessarily because the believer so changed that he is a different person. We have a glimpse of the truth in II Corinthians 5:14, where it is written, "For the love of Christ constraineth us." It is the love of Christ in the believer that moves him out toward other people.

If someone in need should come to your door and you should share with that person, it would not be necessary that you should know him personally. You might not know where he has been nor what he has done nor what he is going to do. All you would need is to be satisfied that the person needs help. The dynamic on your part for doing anything for that needy person will come from the Lord Himself. It will be the love of Christ that constrains you.

When we say the love of Christ constrains us, we are not referring to Christ's emotions. I do not know where the feeling of the Lord in the matter of love is ever described; it is His *action* that is described. The action of the Lord Jesus Christ toward the poor—promising them, healing them, and dying for them—this is our clue. His action inspires action on our part. We have an outlook and an attitude toward all men everywhere which is the way we are prompted from the inside by the love of Christ, which goes out to all men. This is the origin of the frame of mind that enables a person to love his enemies. When the Bible tells us to love our enemies, it is not telling us to like them nor to approve of them. The Bible is showing us, though, that simply because they are creatures of God, we will do for them, we will seek to help them.

The believers in Colossae loved each other. They loved Paul and they loved all men. They had love in their hearts because the love of Christ was in them. How was the love of Christ in them? John will tell you: "Herein is love, not that we loved God, but that he loved us, and sent his Son to be the propitiation for our sins" (I John 4:10). The way in which the love of Christ, exemplified on the cross of Calvary, is going to constrain me is by the Holy Spirit taking the truth of Calvary and showing it to me. If I am faced with the problem of dealing with someone—perhaps a stranger—and I am thinking about it as a believer, I leave my mind and heart open, and the Holy Spirit will bring to my mind that Christ Jesus died for me. If the thought comes to me that this man may not be worthy, the Holy Spirit will remind me I wasn't worthy. All I need to do is to recognize the inward guidance from God that I am to care about the man because this is what He would have me do.

God made all men—they are His; and He has such infinite grace in Him that He would help all people. The fact is that my love in the Spirit, the love that I have toward others, is not derived from other people—this love is grounded in Christ's love for me. He loved me, yes! Then He wants me to love other people. Because He did things for me He wants me to do things for others. This is how the Spirit promotes love in the brethren, among believers. They have it because Christ Jesus loved them.

55

The Gospel Preached by Paul
Was "in the Holy Ghost"

I Thessalonians 1:5

Do you realize that no preacher should ever preach his own ideas?

For our gospel came not unto you in word only, but also in power, and in the Holy Ghost, and in much assurance; as ye know what manner of men we were among you for your sake (I Thess. 1:5).

These are the words of the apostle Paul as he wrote them to the Thessalonian believers. This is a remarkable description of missionary preaching and evangelistic teaching. The gospel as preached by Paul came "in word" surely. There need be no doubt about that! But not in word only; it came also in power.

The preacher of the gospel has a grave responsibility. In only a few cases do people come to hear him personally; they come to hear the gospel. The preacher is expected to know truly what is the will of God, and he is expected to be led in what he has to say, so what he says will actually show forth the things that belong to the will of God. The preacher's big temptation when he preaches is to display his own ideas. Sometimes he does so with pride, he thinks his ideas are so good. Many times he does so almost in desperation because he has no other ideas. The only ones he has are his own. Some who find themselves running short of their own ideas spend a lot of time in books. They come up with excerpts: they read paragraphs and they read poems, some of which may have a very real message, so that the hearer could learn a good deal of truth. Yet this is not quite adequate for the preaching of the gospel.

When the Lord Jesus said, "Go ye into all the world and preach the gospel," He was not thinking primarily that I would go into all the world depending upon either the ideas of others or the procedures of others to convey the truth. I know God can overrule, and God can use anything that suits His purpose. In fact if a preacher did not have anything to say for himself, I sometimes wish he had memorized a good sermon so that when he did say it, at least the sermon would be good and he could transfer it to me. That part of his preaching might be all right. But when he is tempted to figure things out for himself, this is where he runs into danger. You see, a preacher can be conscious of who is sitting before him: he sees his congregation and it is possible he might have enough sense to know what they would like to hear, what would be pleasing in their ears. He realizes that there are ways he could preach what would be flattering to the human nature of his listeners.

Every now and again one can hear some preacher discussing a topic taken from the Bible. He may be commenting on some great hero, some great man or woman in the Bible, and may seem to be taking pleasure in pointing out what he thinks is the limitation of this great person. He seems to be trying to show how very human that person was. No one ever denied that he was human, but those weaknesses and human flaws and blemishes that one may find if one looks for them closely are not actually what the story is all about. That story was written about the fact that God dealt with that person, limited as he may have been.

It is surprising how often in Scripture there are persons in trouble. Men have always been lost and in distress. They were in the days when the young Paul very zealously pursued the religion of the Jews, but he met the Lord Jesus Christ and came to know the grace of the Lord Jesus Christ. Then he went out seeking to save lost souls. The gospel that Paul preached, which was of the Holy Spirit who gave Paul his convictions about Christ and the Holy Spirit, deals with the soul of men: not with his body and not with this world.

This whole truth is to be presented in the Spirit as the preacher declares the mind of Christ. So the preacher, proclaiming this gospel of the Lord Jesus Christ, comes to the individual about his soul. When it is written that "our gospel came unto you not in word only, but also in power, and in the Holy Ghost," you know that he was guided, that the very things he said, the very things he believed and emphasized, were as the Holy Spirit led him to say them. This can be looked for in every Spirit-filled preacher. May God help preachers to be faithful to the inner guidance of the Holy Spirit when they preach the gospel!

56

The Holy Spirit Provides Joy
When a Man Believes

I Thessalonians 1:6

Do you have any idea how it is that a Christian can always rejoice? "A merry heart doeth good like a medicine." That is the way it is written in the Bible, and this is an ordinary comment about a very unusual and happy reality. There are some people who are just naturally cordial; they have good will toward all men. They sympathize with you and are concerned about you; they wish for you the best of everything; they want you to know it, and so they smile at you. What a wonderful thing it is on any given day to meet a smile—I mean, a smiling smile, when people look at you as though they meant you well.

There is an angle to this that is very close to the blessing you receive in the gospel. When you see a person who is cheerful in the presence of other people, is it possible that you are inclined to think that they must have been very fortunate? I wonder if you think that person is cheerful because he has never had trouble. Don't you know people well enough to know better than that? Do you realize that some of the most cheerful people you will ever meet are some with the greatest trouble?

I remember only recently it was my privilege to be in a certain community and I was taken to see a man who was spending his days in an iron lung. It had been years since he had moved under his own strength. For only a few hours a day with special arrangements was he able to be out of that iron lung, yet this man was one of the most cheerful men I have ever met. His face was wreathed in smiles all of the time I was present. How do you account for a thing like that? This man was a real Christian, and he was to me a living demonstration of the fact that a person can be in a smiling condition without being fortunate. There is self-denial in this smile. The person who will smile with you in good will—with the idea of rejoicing with you—is foregoing attention on his own personal circumstances; he is not asking you to think about him; he is, therefore, foregoing self-pity.

When a person looks upon you with good will and smiles at you, that person is not planning to get something out of you; he is not going to impose some sort of tax on your good nature to help him out. It is as though he were saying, "You can relax. I'll not be after you for anything."

If you look around you, you will see people who are ambitious, who want to get ahead. These have a certain kind of smile, different from the smiling smile I have been talking about. You know how to evaluate it—you can pay him just so much for it. I am talking about the person who will greet you with good will, who will be smilingly interested in your affairs. That person is not seeking anything for himself; he is not expecting to be advanced as a consequence of having talked to you; but he would be interested in you and in what you are doing. So I say again, there is thoughtfulness for others in such a smile, there are good wishes for other people, and sympathy for the predicament of others.

When a person comes into a group with a smile, he is as good as saying to the whole group, "I'm not expecting anything from you; I'm not here to get something for me; I'm just here because I'm so glad to be with you and if there is anything I can do to help you out I would be glad to do it." Many a situation is taken care of by fellowship with smiling and cheerful people ready to help.

Let us raise the question, "Will this smiling attitude, this good will, be grounded in a happy disposition?" Some people seem to be born that way: it is just easier for them to be glad than not to be. Sometimes I think there are people who do not fully appreciate the cordiality of their friends because they are ready to think, "Oh, well, he has always been like that; he is just a happy person." Is that the meaning of Scripture when you speak about these people who have joy in the Holy Spirit? No! Does it mean that they have better fortune than other people? No! We can admit there are smiles that come from being fortunate. I have on occasion been very fortunate; I have been in situations when suddenly I was presented with something that was very agreeable to me and I could not forego smiling. I didn't want to stop smiling. I appreciated my good fortune and I felt good toward everybody I met; I could smile at them. But that kind of smiling is not exactly what I have in mind; that is the kind that depends upon my having some temporal benefit of some sort. No, I am talking about something deeper than that. The believer experiences joy which is much deeper than happiness. Joy is actually much deeper than the smile, unless it be the smile in the heart.

The goodwill and joyful outlook of a believer is not based upon anything around him, nor upon anything in his future that he is going to have; it is based actually on what is true above him—out of this world. It is because of the reality of God and of the Lord Jesus Christ and the gospel, because of all the promises of God that have been given to the believer, because of the grace of God that has been shown to him, and because of the joy of the Lord that he has in fellowship with Him. These are the things that make him feel so good and, in a sense, happy about everything; but really and truly, that is joy. While it may show up in the smile and you may just see it in laughter, as it were, actually it has its quiet roots, deep down underneath, in the basic conviction of God's intention to bless and

His intention to keep that which the believer has committed unto Him.

Therefore, a believer may have joy in the midst of distress. He may actually be in the middle of real trouble and yet have joy in the Lord. This is expressed in this verse I want to impress upon you:

. . . having received the word in much affliction, with joy of the Holy Ghost (I Thess. 1:6).

These Thessalonian believers were in trouble, and they were in trouble when they heard the gospel. Whether the trouble came because of the gospel or whether they were in trouble otherwise is not clearly brought out in the account, but what *is* brought out is that when the gospel was preached to them they were in trouble and yet they had joy—the joy of the Holy Spirit.

"Suppose a person is facing real sorrow, perhaps some calamity; can he then actually have joy?" He can because of certain things. The Holy Spirit will remind him of the living Lord Jesus Christ and there may come to him the little song he learned when he was a child, "Jesus loves me, this I know; for the Bible tells me so." He may have that thought go through his mind and there will be a blessing in it. There may also come to his mind the thought that Christ Jesus has died for his sins, and that God has forgiven his sins and will remember them no more against him. He could think of these things. He could also have in mind that he has been reconciled to God. Even though he is weak and undependable, even though he may fall again, if he is willing to receive God's grace and mercy He is willing to share it with him.

In this connection he may have in mind that he has a home in heaven. Sometimes in this world we are filled with great dismay and unhappiness because we think things will never improve, but no matter how things are here, the believer can remember, "Let not your heart be troubled: ye believe in God, believe also in me. In my Father's house are many mansions: if it were not so, I would have told you" (John 14:1-2). And for the joy that is set before him, he can actually live in joy in the Lord.

57

Unclean Conduct Despises the Holy Spirit

I Thessalonians 4:8

Do you realize that wherever a believer goes he is taking the Holy Spirit with him? It is surprising how many believers can forget and ignore that the Holy Spirit is in them. I say it is surprising when you consider how little is said about it.

How many people understand their experience in salvation to be a matter of being delivered from destruction? In other words, they will be saved from going to hell, and they are thankful to God for it, and they will praise Him forever and ever. This is wonderful and true, but it is only the first aspect of the work of salvation. From then on, when a person has been forgiven and has been reconciled to God, the individual is regenerated by the grace of God, and adopted into the family of God. God gives His Holy Spirit into the heart of that person.

Those who believe in the Lord Jesus Christ are given the Holy Spirit to be in them. As we have just said, this is a truth that is seldom emphasized and little discussed so that many Christians innocently grow up without knowing the truth that God has come to dwell in them: "Christ [is] in you." Everybody knows that truth is revealed in the Bible: "Christ in you, the hope of glory." Sometimes it seems to me many take it simply as a figure of speech, as if it were supposed to indicate a sort of general influence. Oh, no! This truth means that the Holy Spirit of God has come to dwell in the heart of the believer. He will take the things of Christ and show them unto the believer. Paul could pray for the Ephesian believers that they might be strengthened by His Spirit in the inner man, that Christ might dwell in their hearts by faith. This is a reality, and this will point up the fact that living in Christ is a daily affair that depends on faith. Christ Jesus belongs to me—morning, noon, and night; at home, in school, and at the office. And I belong to Christ. If I believe it, which is to say I not only admit that it is true as a historic fact, but I count on it being operative in me, then things will follow.

I also will believe that I am to be reckoned dead indeed unto sin. When I reckon myself dead, I have truly denied self. I do not have to do this alone: the Holy Spirit will give me strength. Counting myself to be crucified with Christ, then buried and raised from the dead in Christ means I will yield everything. I yield my problems—He will take care of them; I yield my treasures—He will keep them; I yield everything to Him. I let go and leave all with God. He will raise me into the newness of life, and when God Himself has raised me into newness of life, He will send His Holy Spirit who will dwell in me.

The apostle Paul discusses this in the first epistle to the Corinthians.

> All things are lawful unto me, but all things are not expedient: all things are lawful for me, but I will not be brought under the power of any. Meats for the belly, and the belly for meats: but God shall destroy both it and them. Now the body is not for fornication, but for the Lord; and the Lord for the body. And God hath both raised up the Lord, and will also raise up us by his own power. Know ye not that your bodies are the members of Christ? shall I then take the members of Christ, and make them the members of an harlot? God forbid. What? know ye not that he which is joined to an harlot is one body? for two, saith he, shall be one flesh. But he that is joined unto the Lord is one spirit. Flee fornication. Every sin that a man doeth is without the body; but he that committeth fornication sinneth against his own body (I Cor. 6:12-18).

Now notice these words particularly. "What? know ye not that your body is the temple of the Holy Ghost which is in you, which ye have of God, and ye are not your own? For ye are bought with a price: therefore glorify God in your body, and in your spirit, which are God's" (I Cor. 6:19-20).

Paul is arguing about morality, about how to live. He is saying the reason one should be careful about what one does with one's body is that the Holy Spirit is in it. Paul could have argued that morality was good for you; that it is healthy, economically beneficial, or socially good. He could have argued many things, but in spite of all those reasons a man could yet be immoral. All around us is evidence of that, so Paul brings in a more effective argument. In the believer, right in that body of his, is the Holy Spirit of God. This is a profound truth.

I want to refer you to another passage. "He therefore that despiseth, despiseth not man, but God, who hath also given unto us his holy Spirit" (I Thess. 4:8). Paul had just said before that, "For God hath not called us unto uncleanness, but unto holiness" (I Thess. 4:7). The indication seems to be that what a person does with his body is being done with the Holy Spirit present. For instance, if there is a guest in the house there will be differences in our conduct. If I am all alone in a house I may act in certain ways, doing certain things; but if a person were visiting me I would not allow myself the same liberty of conduct in his presence as I might exercise if I were absolutely alone. I would be more careful, naturally, because I respect that other person. So Paul says that so far as your personal conduct is concerned, be conscious of the fact that the Holy Spirit is with you.

Do you realize that wherever a believer goes he takes the Holy Spirit with him? Whatever a believer does and says, the Holy Spirit is right there with him. This is part of the arrangement of living in Christ, and while you are thinking of the difference between that and the natural man, you will see that it is very effective and in some ways restrictive. When you think about having the Holy Spirit with you, you may say, "Oh, my goodness, I can't do what I want to do." But when your heart is changed and you really want to please God, then the idea of the Holy Spirit with you is a real comfort because everything He moves you to do will be pleasing in God's sight. If your heart is right with God you will want to please God anyway, so the more you can have the Holy Spirit with you, that much stronger will be the disposition to please God. For that reason you will thank God for giving you the Holy Spirit.

58

The Holy Spirit Should Not Be Quenched

I Thessalonians 5:19

Do you understand that a person can silence the voice of God in his own soul? We have been studying about the Holy Spirit and suddenly this truth has never seemed as important as it is now. It seems to me when I talk about the Holy Spirit in the soul, in the heart of a believer, that I am discussing *all* about the Christian life. Living in the Holy Spirit, by the Holy Spirit, with the Holy Spirit is actually all that is involved in living in Christ.

We cannot live in Christ except by the Holy Spirit of God who is in us. It is by the Holy Spirit that we are able to live and to walk in and with Christ Jesus. The truth of the matter is that so far as the believer is concerned, it is God Himself who worketh in him, to will and to do of His good pleasure. How is this done? This is the work of the Holy Spirit showing the things of Christ in the heart of the believer, in the consciousness of the believer—affecting him in such a way that he is moved into the will of the Lord Jesus Christ.

The Lord Jesus Christ is a living being; and the Holy Spirit unites me to the Lord in a living way, as a hand or a foot is united to the head. Whatever the head wills done, my hand or my foot does, and I have just such a relationship with the Lord Jesus Christ in the Holy Spirit. I am actually related to Him in such a way that his will is what moves me to action. It is true that I have ideas of my own, and I have my own limitations, and this causes me to drag my feet many times; yet it is God who worketh in me, to will and to do—to actually move me to want to do the right thing and then to get it done.

When a great preacher, eloquent in the Spirit, is actually pronouncing the truth of the gospel in a powerful way one could say that he is filled with the Spirit. And when that word reaches my own heart and soul I could think the Spirit of God is certainly working in him. True, but the truth of the matter goes further than that. In all situations of living in faith this great truth is operative: God Himself has given the Holy Spirit to be in you, day by day, hour by hour, minute by minute, in anything and everything you will ever do as a child of God.

The Holy Spirit can make me conscious of the things of the Lord Jesus Christ, remembering which will bless me. In my daily work, whatever it might be, God wants me as a believer to be aware that the Lord Jesus Christ is with me all the time. I do not have to be in any special place; the Lord will be present with me as I walk in my faith in Christ: He will be in my heart. If I am a student I can tell you that inasmuch as I belong to the Lord Jesus Christ, the Holy Spirit is going to be in my heart and by my side all day long. I know He will be with the missionaries; I know He will be with the preachers and with the people who are in real trouble, and with those who are dying.

I can have the joy of the Lord in my soul as I walk down the street, just allowing my heart to be aware of the fact that Christ Jesus Himself is walking with me. Sometimes people are disagreeable, and situations may be hard. I may be face to face with all manner of difficulties; but the Lord Jesus Himself will be with me because His Holy Spirit indwells me. Any time—all the time—the Spirit comes to all believers. The Spirit is meek and humble—He will come anywhere. He does not hold a grudge. He is ready to come.

There is one other truth that I should emphasize: the Holy Spirit is wonderfully kind to us at all times; but He will not tolerate evil. In other words, when I am living in the presence of God and I want the Holy Spirit to be with me, should I act willfully it will offend Him; it will quench Him. If I am careless and thoughtless, it will quench Him; if I am indifferent to Him who has done so much for me, that can cause Him to be quiet; and if I am proud or selfish or highminded, if I am envious of other people or jealous or try to make something of myself at the expense of my fellowman, if I give myself over to the works of the flesh, I hurt His feelings. I can quench the Holy Spirit of God until I can silence the voice of God in my soul. It will be a dark night when the light goes out. May God forbid!